500

Tips for Trainers

Also from Kogan Page

500 Tips on Assessment Sally Brown, Phil Race and Brenda Smith
500 Computing Tips for Teachers Phil Race and Steve McDowell
500 Tips for Research Students Liz McDowell, Phil Race and Sally Brown
500 Tips for Teachers Sally Brown, Carolyn Earlam and Phil Race
500 Tips for Tutors Phil Race and Sally Brown

500

Tips for Trainers

**PHIL RACE AND
BRENDA SMITH**

KOGAN
PAGE

First published in 1995
Reprinted 1996 (twice)

Kogan Page Limited
120 Pentonville Road
London N1 9JN

British Library Cataloguing in Publication Data

A CIP record for this book is available from the British Library.

ISBN 0 7494 1591 6

Typeset by Saxon Graphics Ltd, Derby
Printed and bound in Great Britain by Biddles Ltd, Guildford and King's Lynn

Contents

Introduction

We've written this book for busy people! We know that if you're a busy trainer, you probably won't have much time (or appetite) for the sort of book which offers profound and deep theories of how people learn at training sessions, or complex pedagogical models of how we should try to structure our training. In this book we've tried to offer down-to-earth, practical suggestions.

We've designed this book as a dip-in resource. We don't expect anyone to read it cover to cover. We've tried to build in a sort of logic, with planning towards the start of the book and evaluating towards the end, but many of the sets of suggestions could have been placed in different chapters and in a different sequence, so don't regard the order of presentation of our suggestions as definitive!

On the whole, we've presented ten tips on each of 50 topics (except that a couple of times we got over-enthused and ended up with 20, even 22, tips instead of ten!). At the start of each collection of tips, we've added a line or two to help you see what the suggestions are really about; we hope these introductions will help you to decide which sets of tips to have a look at – and which to skip or save for later!

We're quite sure that when you look at some of our suggestions you'll say to yourself, 'Yes, but I already do this!' This is of course fine. Our main hope is that you'll also find something that makes you say to yourself, 'Ah, I've never tried that – I may be able to give it a go in my next session.'

We'd like to have your reactions to our book. We've added a short questionnaire at the end of the book, and we will be delighted if you would fill this in and send it care of our publishers. We will be pleased to acknowledge in the next edition of this book any suggestions you give us.

Phil Race
Brenda Smith
March 1995

Chapter 1 Planning and Preparation

1 What do you want to be the nature of your training events?
2 Setting training event objectives
3 Getting the content right
4 Timetabling your training events
5 Advertising your training event
6 Tips when using visiting trainers
7 Designing pre-event tasks
8 Behind the scenes
9 Refreshments

In this chapter we take a look at things to do with planning and preparing your training events, and also include suggestions for putting into practice your planning when running training events. Several of the ideas we introduce in this chapter are expanded on in suggestions in the remainder of this book. We have discovered how dangerous it can be to imagine that we've run a particular session so often that we can afford to skip some of the detail of preparing the ground in advance.

For a start, we think that it's worth thinking about exactly what we mean by a 'training event'. If everyone expects a training event session to be interactive, participant-centred, and not just a lecture or presentation, we think that such training events are more likely to be effective than when no one knows quite what to expect.

We move on next to consider the intended outcomes of training event sessions. Participants want to know – and need to know – what is likely to be expected of them in our sessions. One of the best ways to let participants know exactly what is expected is to formulate the training event outcomes in the form of objectives.

Obviously, the content of your training events is important. However, perhaps even more important are the processes and methods by which you deliver your training events. Our advice boils down to suggesting that you consider how best you can turn the theoretical or practical content of your training events into learning resources which participants use during your sessions, and activities which they engage with during the sessions.

We cannot overestimate the importance of running to time. When a training event falls behind schedule, everyone feels uncomfortable. Perhaps the secret is to have schedules which are in practice sufficiently flexible to allow us as facilitators to make gentle adjustments to the programme without any-one feeling that they are being rushed or that things are being omitted.

Sometimes, the success of your training event will depend on how well you advertise it. One of the key points is to make your sessions appear really attractive and relevant to the people you regard as your ideal target audience.

Sometimes you'll be using visiting trainers to run training events for your own people. We've learned that it's worth paying attention to how we make best use of such colleagues, and have wrapped up what we have learned in the form of some suggestions you can adapt to your own situation.

One way of getting a training event off to a good start is to make sure that everyone has done some preparatory work. We give some suggestions for pre-event tasks, which can help to focus your training events on the important issues rather than filling in background detail.

Many of the little preparations which ensure the smooth running of training events could be said to take place 'behind the scenes'. We provide some general tips based on our own experiences (unsuccessful as well as successful) at setting-up a good training event environment.

Human beings require feeding and watering! We regard refreshments as just as important a part of our training events as anything we try to do our-selves. When refreshments are punctual, appropriate and good, the whole atmosphere of a training event is improved considerably, and leaves partici-pants with the memory of a very pleasant taste!

1

What do you want to be the nature of your training events?

In this book, we're sharing ideas to help make training events active learning experiences, and not just 'sit, watch and listen' occasions. It is a useful start to plan into the design of your training events several features and characteristics. We suggest some ideas below.

1 **A training event should be an active occasion for participants, not just for us!** It's well worth building your training event programmes around the things that participants will do during the sessions. People tend to remember more when they are actively involved – and having fun!

2 **Plan each training event like a journey, with a beginning, a middle and a goal.** This helps you to ensure that training events are a coherent learning experience for participants, and that they know where they are at each stage.

3 **Participants need to know where they're going.** Make the purposes of each training event as clear as possible, for example by spelling out intended learning outcomes or training event objectives.

4 **Participants want to know why they should be going.** Express the intended learning outcomes in terms which participants will find relevant to their work situations, and attractive targets for them personally.

5 **Participants like to know how they will get there.** Share with participants information about the sorts of processes they will engage in during the various stages of a training event – doing so may help to dispel any anxieties.

6 **Regard the experience of your participants as your greatest training event resource.** Whenever possible, allow participants to tell you things, rather than you telling them things that some of them may already know. Give participants credit for what they already know whenever possible.

7   **Build in interaction whenever possible.** A good training event is mainly interactive, and uses only a very limited amount of 'direct input' from trainers. The input does not have to be in presentation format, but can take the form of learning resources such as handouts, displays and case studies.

8   **Allow for ongoing feedback from participants.** It is far better to abandon your original plans when something unexpected but important crops up, than to try to soldier on and stick to a preplanned schedule of what should be covered in a training event. However, don't abandon coffee breaks!

9   **Anticipate 'what I would like participants to say about this training event'.** Try to plan your training events along lines that will be both enjoyable and productive from their point of view.

10 **Regard each training event as a new learning experience for yourself.** The day you think you've got a training event 'exactly right', you've got a problem! If that day comes, design some different training events, and keep on learning!

2

Setting training event objectives

People like to know where they're heading. They like to know what they may expect to be able to do at the end of the training session that they can't do already, or that they may like to do better. They also like to know how the things they can already do relate to the agenda for the session. It is therefore crucial to be clear about the intended learning outcomes of training sessions.

1 **Look for likely 'training needs'.** In pre-event planning, talk to anyone who can help you focus on the real issues that you should attempt to cover during the forthcoming training session.

2 **Start with some 'provisional' objectives.** Prepare an overhead transparency (or handout sheet) listing some relatively broad 'intended outcomes' of your training session.

3 **Ask participants, 'What do you want?'** Asking participants to identify their own personal wishes helps you to find out the 'real agenda' that may lie behind the training session. A good way of doing this is to give out small pieces of acetate (or post-its) and ask participants to write down what they 'hope for most' from the forthcoming session.

4 **Treat participants' wishes seriously.** If you have gone to the trouble of collecting participants' expectations, don't waste them. Stick them up on a flipchart where they can remain visible throughout the training session. As often as possible, return to particular participants' expectations as the session progresses.

5 **Get the wording right.** Make sure that the words used to express training objectives or intended learning outcomes mean the same to everyone. Ask, 'What do we really mean by this?' and adjust the wording so that the objectives are understood and shared by all present.

6 **Feel free to jettison some of your own objectives.** When the real agenda (as determined from participants) differs from the agenda which you prepared in your planning for a training session, it is important to be seen to be willing to favour participants' wishes, even at the expense of some training event objectives which you yourself feel are really valuable.

7 **Try getting participants to prioritize objectives or outcomes.** For example, suppose there are six possible objectives. Ask participants to give each of the objectives a 'star rating', such as 'three stars for crucial', 'two stars for useful', 'one star for interesting', 'zero stars for irrelevant'. Collect up the 'stars' on a flipchart or overhead listing the objectives, and take your priorities from the result.

8 **Return to the objectives or intended outcomes.** Link training event activities to the objectives, so that your participants can see exactly why they are being asked to do particular things during the training session.

9 **At the end, review the objectives or intended outcomes.** Feel free to admit those that have not been achieved by the session. Confirm those that you know have been addressed successfully.

10 **At the very end, return to your participants' expectations.** Give them the opportunity to confirm which of their expectations have been realized during the training session and which still remain as 'outstanding'. It is often possible to harness the 'outstanding' expectations as the basis for a follow-up training session.

3

Getting the content right

Many of the suggestions in our book are about *how* to conduct training events, rather than about *what* to cover in them. Of course, the content itself is important too. We hope the following ideas will prove useful.

1 **Link the content of your training event directly to the advertised aims or objectives.** Of every component of your planned training event, ask yourself, 'How exactly does this relate to the intended outcomes?' If the link is tenuous, the element concerned may be an optional extra.

2 **Remember that most activities take longer than we imagine they will.** This is particularly important when devising new activities that you haven't tried out before. It is better to allow 45 minutes for such an activity, then fill in with something else if it only takes 30 minutes, than vice versa.

3 **Don't ride hobby-horses too hard!** When we've got a strong belief in something, it's all too easy for us to plug it so hard that it becomes difficult for participants to take – particularly if they have views rather different to ours.

4 **Research how relevant and useful each part of your training event feels to participants.** In follow-up questionnaires or interviews, ask which parts of the training event content were most useful, and ask which things could be left out if necessary.

5 **Give participants your content rather than tell them it.** It can save a great deal of time to have the main principles of your training event wrapped up in handout materials or summaries, so that participants can spend their time with you exploring the issues rather than trying to write them down.

6 **Check that your content is authoritative, up-to-date and correct.** It is very useful to find trusted colleagues elsewhere who will be willing to look at your handout materials and overheads with a supportive but critical eye, and give you feedback about anything that may need to be adjusted.

7 **Remember that content changes.** Participants will regard your training event as being as up-to-date as the most recent developments you refer to during the session. Make sure you have some new references as well as well-established ones. A handout sheet listing these is very much appreciated.

8 **Let participants help you to develop your content.** Next month's repeat session can benefit a lot by incorporating questions and answers which emerge from your present training event. A sheet collecting together such questions and answers is very useful as handout material for future training events.

9 **Focus on what participants will do during your training event.** The activities you devise will be the most important aspect of your participants' view of the content of your training event.

10 **Have plenty of spare 'content' up your sleeve!** You never know when an activity will take only half the time you allowed for it (for example when everyone already knows a lot about the subject). Sometimes, you'll have to drop a training event element entirely because you find out at the last minute that everyone has already covered it elsewhere. Have ready a range of alternative things that you can use to fill participants' time usefully.

4

Timetabling your training event

If you can manage time, you can manage everything else. Timetabling a training event is an important element of designing it. We've gathered the following ideas by trial and error – mostly by error!

1 **Start with coffee (and tea, and juice!).** For example, you're much more likely to achieve a prompt 10.15 start if the advertised programme starts with 'Coffee, and informal introductions' at 09.45.

2 **Start on time anyway.** Even if participants are still drifting in for an assortment of wonderful reasons, it does no harm to be seen to be already under way at the advertised start time. You can choose to do things that aren't particularly important until everyone has arrived. If you delay the start, participants who have made the effort to be punctual can feel very cheated!

3 **Stop on time (or even ahead of time) for coffee breaks or meal breaks.** It may come as a great disappointment to you that most participants are actually rather pleased when a coffee break starts five minutes early!

4 **Don't say 'come back in 20 minutes'.** No one will know when the 20 minutes started! It's more effective to say 'Please can we resume at 11.23?' (An odd time tends to stick in people's memories, and usually works surprisingly well.)

5 **Plan a reasonable amount of time for coffee breaks.** As well as consuming a drink and a biscuit, participants will probably want to pay a call – or make a call. Also, the conversations that participants get into during breaks are not only interesting but useful. It's better to have a prompt start after a 25-minute break than a laboured start after an attempt at a 15-minute break.

6 **Sometimes, avoid breaks, but still have coffee.** Where refreshments are available in the room, it is then possible to give 'five minutes' for everyone to equip themselves with refreshments, and enter into (for example) a plenary discussion or syndicate task where participants can consume their refreshments as they work.

7 **Don't underestimate how long it takes for everyone to get lunch!** Even when running training events in hotels, there may be slow table-service, or queues at the buffet table. (Pull out the buffet table from the wall which it always seems to be placed against, so that participants have twice the opportunity of serving themselves!)

8 **In case lunch is fast, ensure that participants don't have a boring wait.** One way of doing this is to combine lunch with a lunchtime task, or an exhibition of materials, so that participants can use any spare time without feeling held-up.

9 **Have a clearly advertised finishing time.** This helps participants plan round the other things in their lives, including transport home, or picking up kids from school. *Always* finish on (or ahead of) this time. You can of course stay on for informal chats with those participants who are not in any hurry after 'closing time'.

10 **Don't try to do everything you've prepared for.** When a training event gets 'behind your personal schedule', feel free to drop inputs or activities that are not crucial, and aim to give every appearance of sticking to the planned timetable. Remember, participants find the words, 'I don't think we need to spend any further time on this – we've already explored it quite fully this morning' music to their ears!

5

Advertising your training event

Think how you can reach your potential audience, and persuade them to attend your training event.

1   **Use a catchy title.** Be creative – but be honest. Brainstorm with your friends and try out a few suggested titles with your colleagues.

2   **Whom do you want to attend?** Work out exactly what sort of people you believe can benefit from your training event, and adjust the title and content of your planned training event to be relevant to their needs.

3   **Say what you're about.** When describing the content and aims of your training event or course, try to give as full a description as space will allow.

4   **Indicate how it will go.** Let potential participants see in advance whether your programme will be interactive rather than just sitting-and-listening, use role plays or simulations, involve small-group activities, involve follow-up actions. Also indicate whether participants may need to do some prior preparations before they attend.

5   **Plan your advertising.** Decide how you will advertise your programme to get the best possible responses from potential participants. (Don't worry about being oversubscribed – it is a delight to need to run a second or third training event at later dates to meet needs.)

6   **Advertise in several modes.** For example, try
    - in-house magazines
    - professional organization journals
    - national journals that often permit free advertisements
    - direct contact with people such as heads of department, section leaders, network groups, on notice-boards, in the local library, by e-mail, by personal contact with colleagues and at any opportunity over the phone.

7 **Be colourful and creative!** Advertise on paper of a striking or unusual colour. Colleagues will often remember the blue sheet buried in that pile of papers in the office. However, there's a risk that you'll be accused of 'rainbow training' if you overdo the colour! Use of appropriate graphics can be eye-catching, and can make the whole training event appear more professional.

8 **Advertise well in advance.** More and more people have busy diaries. It is usually the busiest people that you really wish to attract to your training events.

9 **Think globally.** Remember that people from abroad visit your country on holidays, business trips or sabbaticals. Try to tap in to international networks.

10 **Watch your competition.** Start collecting details of how other training events and courses are advertised and promoted. You can learn a lot from your competitors.

6

Tips when using visiting trainers

It is always a good idea to introduce variety and change by inviting outside trainers or speakers. However famous and well-respected these people are, a few guidelines can be vital!

1 **Agree things in writing.** A friendly conversation over the telephone may be difficult to recall months or even weeks later. It is useful therefore to put pen to paper and send a summary of your conversation to visiting trainers.

2 **Check the understanding of the title.** The same words can all too easily mean different things to different people at different times! Try to check out exactly what the title means to you, and to the visiting trainer. Talk things over in advance.

3 **Discuss in some detail the areas to be covered.** Have you had an experience where you thought you had agreed something, only to find the other person doing or saying something completely different? It can be embarrassing, especially when you see the looks on other people's faces. Talk through exactly what you both understand about the topics to be covered. Examples can be very useful.

4 **Prepare guidance notes about overhead transparencies.** How many times have we all been at training events where we cannot read what is shown on the overhead projector? A few guidance notes on general layout and size of print can save much embarrassment later. Prepare a standard checklist form to send to all visiting speakers – this could help maintain the quality of your training provision.

5 **Ensure that enough copies of handouts are available for distribution.** Ask presenters to bring along copies of their overhead transparencies, or send them before the event, so that you can produce copies. Suggest shrinking overheads to four or six on a page, and photocopy on both sides of the paper to save forests.

6 **Check when your presenter wants to distribute material.** If handouts are supplied in advance, check whether it is intended that they should be issued at the start, or at particular stages during the session.

7 **Check what facilities the presenter will need.** Ask how the room should be set out. Are tables needed for materials? Is a remote control for the video essential or not? Someone who wishes to stop and start a video frequently while adding comments could be rather thrown if they have to sit in front of the machine and jump up and down at each appropriate moment.

8 **Send a good map, well in advance.** There is nothing more frustrating than trying to find a venue with a poorly constructed map, especially when doing so as a visiting presenter. Ensure the map is printed large enough to read without a magnifying glass, and that appropriate buildings and streets are clearly marked. It is a good idea to indicate which way the map should be held, by relating it to marked buildings or landmarks, and always include a compass pointer which shows which way 'North' is at least – otherwise it is all too easy to hold a map upside down!

9 **Don't be afraid to interject when necessary.** If you can see that the audience has completely switched off, try to bring the session back on track. Throwing in a question can help to steer things in another direction when necessary, or can help the audience to understand better. Alternatively, a quick and friendly chat to the visiting trainer over coffee can often save the day.

10 **Follow up with a thank-you note.** However experienced we are, it is always good to receive such notes. It may also be appropriate to send on any evaluation comments you receive.

7

Designing pre-event tasks

You haven't always the chance to set participants tasks to do in preparation for a training event – but when such an opportunity is available, you can use it to your advantage, and your participants can benefit considerably too. Here are some suggestions.

1 **Make sure the tasks reach everyone in good time.** One way of checking that all your participants have received the tasks is for the same mailing to include something they need to send back to you before the training event – for example a registration form, or a car-parking permit request.

2 **Don't make the tasks too demanding.** Short, specific tasks are best. Ideally, you want all participants to have spent approximately equal time on the tasks, rather than have some participants who have spent a great deal of effort on them while others have only thought about them lightly.

3 **Include pro-formas.** For example, if one of your tasks is, 'Work out a list of ten questions that you think we should address during the course of the training event', providing a page with ten boxes can help to make sure that participants bring their lists ready. They can then be displayed during the training event, and an agenda for discussion can be made from the most common questions.

4 **Make the tasks quite definite.** It's little use just asking participants to read through some handout material as preparation for the training event. It is better to give them something definite to do while they read, such as, 'find five advantages of the approach described in the handout, and also find five drawbacks.'

5 **Use the tasks to bring participants up to an appropriate 'starting level'.** It can save a lot of valuable time if those participants who are starting from scratch have an opportunity to gain familiarity with the basics of the topic from tasks they do using handout materials before they come to the event itself.

6 **Use pre-event tasks to prioritize training event objectives or outcomes.** Simply asking participants to give a rating showing which objectives or outcomes they can already achieve is useful. This can help you wasting time on things that your participants can already do.

7 **Don't depend on all participants having done your pre-event tasks.** With the best will in the world, things won't always go your way. You may end up with one or two substitute participants who were told to attend your training event at the last minute – and of course, they won't even know about the pre-event tasks.

8 **Don't leave a task unattended.** When people have spent time doing some preparation, they are naturally quite upset if their work goes unrecognized. Make sure that each pre-event task is debriefed at least briefly during the training event.

9 **Encourage participants to bring along to the training event materials they think may be useful or relevant.** Setting a pre-event task along these lines may help you track down valuable resource materials that you would not have come across otherwise, and such tasks place value on participants' existing knowledge and experience.

10 **Print your pre-event task sheets on coloured paper.** This can help you recognize at once the things that participants have already done in preparation – and it helps participants themselves to avoid losing the task sheets in a mass of white papers.

8

Behind the scenes

It's vital that you make due preparations before your training event takes place, so that everyone is at ease during the session – and to save you from last-minute panics.

1 **Get your venue details right – and send them out.** Send each participant relevant details, including travel directions if needed, about ten days ahead of the event. Remember that some participants may be travelling directly from some other event or location, so allow time for the details to be redirected to them if necessary.

2 **Show the way.** Prepare large direction signs for the event and venue – enough for all possible entrances to the building. Remember how creative people can be when it comes to finding their way into a building they do not know!

3 **Prepare name badges for everyone (including yourself).** These are best prepared using big lettering (18- or 24-point on desk-top-publishing programmes) so that names can be seen without an intimate inspection of the upper body! Double-check your spelling of people's names – no one likes to be misnamed.

4 **Feed bodies as well as minds.** Check that catering arrangements are in place and that you have catered for diverse needs or tastes as far as you can. If you want to keep your group awake in the afternoon, fresh fruit works rather better than syrup sponge and custard. However, oranges (except mandarin) are not a good idea, as participants don't really want to be seen with juice dripping down their fronts!

5 **Prepare evaluation sheets.** Make these specific to the event you're going to run, so that you can gather detailed feedback on which of the aims have been achieved successfully, and find out any expectations that have not been met.

6 **Check your equipment!** Make sure that you are familiar with the projector, video-machine or TV sets that you may want to use during your session.

7 **Get your ambience sorted out.** For example, if you wish to play suitable music during the minutes while participants are arriving and settling in, check that suitable playback equipment is available – it's often worth bringing your own anyway (a small portable tape or disc machine will do).

8 **Have more than enough handouts.** Check that they are stapled in the correct order, or filed in piles so that you can give them out in the right order as your session proceeds. Photocopy or print back-to-back wherever possible, to save trees.

9 **Get your own act together in advance.** Get your overheads and notes assembled into the right order, so that you don't have to scrabble around looking for particular resources as you proceed.

10 **Know who is supposed to be coming.** Get your list of expected participants ready, and have copies available for everyone. When participants are coming from around the country, it can be useful to circulate lists in advance, including contact phone numbers, so that participants can help each other with travel arrangements. It is amazing how often participants can travel to your session from the same site and organization, without knowing of each other's attendance until they arrive!

9

Refreshments

The best way to a person's heart (notice our adherence to equal opportunities principles here!) is through the person's stomach. We've mentioned refreshments more than once in other sets of tips in this book, but this time we wish to concentrate on feeding the inner person.

1 **Provide drinks on arrival.** People may have travelled a long way and usually welcome a top-up of caffeine, tannin and so on. Try to arrange that the drinks are available some time before the advertised start of the session, so that people who arrive early have their own reward.

2 **Allow people to make choices.** Provide tea (herbal, raspberry, orange, passion fruit), coffee, orange juice, hot water, cold water, fizzy water or plain water. People feel better when they have choices to make. This is your first step towards empowering your participants. Making such choices is also a good way of participants getting to know you and each other.

3 **Don't forget the late arrivals.** Make sure that the drinks are still available 30 minutes after the start of your programme. Anything could have happened that morning – failed alarm clock, flat tyre, mother-in-law called just before departure, late train, and so on. It's not always people's fault when they're late. (In your case, of course, it is your fault!)

4 **Provide lots of refreshments.** Regular breaks help the brain to function more effectively and it's amazing what some people will tell you over a cup of coffee!

5 **Provide a table for the refreshments.** Those with bad backs will find difficulty bending down to floor level to pick up their cup of tea. A table also acts as a central focus for conversation. It somehow gives stability to strangers, and if anyone finds conversation difficult, they can always eat a biscuit and talk about the advantages of wholemeal ones.

6   **Place the table in a suitable part of the room.** If the refreshments are to be topped-up throughout the event, try to avoid the catering staff having to fight their way through people, chairs, flipcharts and video-cameras. Place the table somewhere where it is easily accessible, and not blocking anyone's view. If your group is large it helps to place the table so that people can get to all sides of it – this helps to avoid queues.

7   **Watch the budget.** It is really impressive to serve fresh salmon and strawberries, followed by afternoon tea! However, you may be unable to provide seminars later in the year, or people may not be able to afford to come. Simple wholesome food also helps to keep people awake!

8   **Variety is the spice of life.** Isn't it amazing how different we all are? Have you ever tried cooking a meal for six children!! In your group you will probably have 'normal' folk, vegetarians, demi-vegetarians, lacto-vegetarians, wholemeal bread lovers, those that can't eat pork, eggs, caviar, cucumber and so on. Play safe and provide a mixture of food.

9   **Provide earplugs or play lively music!** Have you ever wondered why catering staff never go on training courses which teach them how to lay out cups and saucers quietly? Try and be flexible so that while stocks are being replenished you can provide a change in activity which does not require quiet contemplation.

10 **Allow lots of time for eating.** Evaluations often state that the most valuable part of the session was talking to colleagues. Therefore a way of improving your ratings with clients is to provide lots of opportunity for this interaction to occur. How often have you had to leave a lovely sticky dessert because the afternoon session was about to begin?

Chapter 2 Getting Participants Going

Especially when running training events for people you don't already know, there's no second chance for you to make a good first impression! It's also important to set the tone well in the way you introduce yourself to your participants. It's also a good idea to help participants to get to know each other in a way that will help them to interact productively together in your sessions. Therefore our first three sets of tips in this chapter are all about getting your training event off to a good start.

We next move to ideas on ways to find out exactly what your participants may want from your sessions. There may indeed be a gap between what they want, what they need – and what you had intended to do with them! However, armed with their expectations for your sessions, you may be surprised just how possible it often is to steer the sessions towards things that participants want, as well as covering what is intended to be covered by the programme. This makes for happier participants, and therefore more productive and more successful training events.

We all know the adage that starts with the words, 'You can lead a horse to water, but. . .'. Probably the most important factor when we run training events is whether our participants really *want* to learn from our sessions. There is no magic way of ensuring that people want to learn – but we share some tips based on our experiences of trying out a number of ways to generate or amplify such a want.

Often, trainers set participants pre-event tasks to help them all to focus on the topic of the training events, and to bring them all to a common base of experience or knowledge. We have learned the hard way how bitter participants can feel if we fail to follow-up pre-event tasks in a tangible way during the actual sessions. No one likes to feel they have done something they did not need to do.

In many kinds of training events, it is useful to clarify exactly what participants may be expected to be able to do as a result of participating. Expressing the intended outcomes in terms of performance criteria and evidence indicators can go a long way towards helping participants to see the relevance and importance of the skills, attributes and knowledge they are intended to develop as a result of training events.

To gain participants' full cooperation during a training event (particularly a long training event or a series of shorter ones) it is often worth engaging with them to negotiate a learning contract. This allows them to clarify exactly what they may expect us to do, as well as to firm up their own aims and objectives.

Brainstorming, in one form or another, is a very useful way of bringing in the knowledge and experience of participants, so that the training event avoids telling them things they already know, and acknowledges and builds on their existing expertise.

10

First impressions count

There is no second chance to make a good first impression! When people first arrive at a training event they are often feeling a little bit apprehensive. Anything you can do to put them at their ease helps.

1 **Tell people where to go!** Make sure participants know which room the session will be in, and where the toilets are. Put up signs around the building, and be prepared for some participants to arrive via side doors!

2 **Welcome participants.** Putting up a 'welcome' overhead slide, or a 'welcome' message on the flipchart, can help participants to settle in comfortably.

3 **Be there as participants arrive.** Smile and welcome them individually – this is a good time to start your task of learning their names. Resist any temptation to sit there finishing your preparations, or reading the newspaper, however desperate you are to catch up on the news!

4 **Feed your participants!** Have refreshments waiting – not just tea and coffee, but orange juice and hot water for the non-caffeine addicts or herbal tea-drinkers. The health-food culture is here to stay!

5 **Chat to participants informally as they arrive.** There's plenty to chat about, including the weather, late trains, burst tyres, British Rail coffee, and the effect of the climate on gardens. Don't declare your political sympathies yet, however!

6 **Move around and address participants by name.** Check that they have their name badges on (and maybe also supply name cards so everyone can see each other's names at a considerable distance). Ensure that first names can be seen easily, and try to encourage Mr A G Jones to relax enough for everyone to be able to call him 'Archie'!

7 **Be comfortable yourself.** Choose your own clothes so that you can look comfortable and confident, even though your knees may be shaking! Check in advance your buttons or zips – otherwise people who notice any discrepancies may stare at you unmercifully!

8 **Get the venue ambience right.** A bowl or vase of flowers can make a stark training room look homely. However, check that participants can see past such artefacts – and place them where you're not going to send them flying as you make a gesture of emphasis!

9 **Make the venue sound interesting.** Having baroque or mood music playing softly in the background can help participants relax and settle in.

10 **Keep your cool! (or warm!)** Check that the temperature of the room is moderate, and find out how to control it. Be prepared to monitor and adjust the room temperature throughout your session. Remember to ask participants now and then whether they feel it is too stuffy or too cool, and so on.

11

Introducing yourself

Whenever working with a new group of participants, you need to introduce yourself in one way or another. The following suggestions may help you decide how to do this on particular occasions.

1 **Circulate a brief cv beforehand.** This can list your areas of experience and also give details of the particular aspects of training that you're normally involved in. It's worth making this sort of cv friendly rather than intimidating – a bit about your likes and dislikes does no harm!

2 **Prepare an overhead to introduce you.** This can give brief details of your background or experience and alert your participants to some aspects of the style in which you will conduct the course. Be careful, however, not to read out to participants word-for-word things they can see on the screen. Elaborate on one or two points where appropriate.

3 **Tell it all verbally.** This is probably the option we recommend least! Not many participants really enjoy hearing the life history of their facilitators. However, there may be times when you find that you should choose this option. Don't forget, though, that participants won't actually remember much of something they simply hear – they will only remember the impression (or lack of one) that the words made.

4 **Make it clear through pre-event documentation.** Including things you have already written or published in pre-event papers can be a useful way of alerting participants to your track record in the field.

5 **Be interviewed by participants.** This can be an interesting way for participants to find out more about you (and for you to find out a great deal about them). Suggest that groups of participants spend a few minutes formulating questions about you, your background and your experience, then stand ready to deliver answers to their questions.

6 **Get yourself introduced.** Sometimes, your client may be willing to provide an introduction to the person who is about to facilitate a training session. You may well need to provide your client with succinct briefing notes to keep this introduction to the areas that you wish to be covered! Alternatively, you may be lucky enough to be quite embarrassed by the eloquence of such an introduction.

7 **Make little introduction at all.** Sometimes it is best to let participants get to know you as your course unfolds, and to make no claims regarding experience or expertise, particularly if you have a lot of either.

8 **Get everyone to introduce themselves.** You can then join in along with the rest, giving a few choice words about your background and experience.

9 **Don't do a hard sell!** If you're famous in your field, there's no benefit in advertising your latest books during the introduction! In fact, advertising your own work at the beginning of a training event can alienate participants irrevocably. If you're so famous, everyone will already know of your work.

10 **Concentrate on beliefs or values.** Get everyone to introduce themselves in terms of what they believe in or value, and join in with them.

12

Introducing participants

How participants at your training events first get to know each other can make a big difference to the progress of your sessions. Here are some ideas about ensuring that participants learn about each other.

1 **Keep introductions in perspective!** For example, when starting off a five-day training event, extended introductions can be worthwhile, but in a half-day event, for example, it's very important to keep them short.

2 **Do a round of 'who I am, and what I believe in.'** This can give participants the chance to explain their background, but also to express their points of view regarding the theme of the session.

3 **Get participants to interview each other in pairs.** Then ask everyone to give a brief introduction about the person they have just interviewed. This has the benefit of allowing participants' achievements to be aired by someone else, and preserves modesty.

4 **Devise a pro-forma.** Ask all participants to fill in details of their background, views, and experience, and then ask all to display their pro formas on a wall.

5 **'One thing I really like...' (or 'One thing I really hate...' – or both).** Ask all participants to identify such things, and to say a few words about themselves in the context of whatever they choose to reveal about themselves under this category.

6 **'What I really want from this course, and why'.** This is a way of letting participants state their personal expectations, and also to give some details of the circumstances surrounding their expectations of your course.

7   '**Four things in common**'. Provide a checklist covering a range of inter-
    ests, hobbies, beliefs and values. Ask participants to tick up to six things
    that apply to them individually. Then ask them to compare their
    responses to other people, and identify fellow-participants where, say,
    four things are 'in common' on their lists. This can help to bring
    together kindred spirits at the start of a course.

8   **Introduce a treasure-hunt.** For example, devise a sheet with some of
    the following questions, asking group members to find someone else in
    the room with, for example:

    - the same colour eyes
    - blue as a favourite colour
    - a penchant for pasta
    - roses as favourite flowers
    - a wish to holiday in the Caribbean.

    - a talent for singing in the bath
    - a cat
    - a liking for walking over open fields
    - a liking for talking books

    Each person 'discovered' is asked to place their name on the lists along-
    side the appropriate preferences.

9   **Draw a poster.** Put participants in pairs and ask them to share their
    likes and dislikes (and anything else they don't mind sharing with the
    rest of the group). Then ask them to draw a poster together depicting
    some information they have just shared. See if the rest of the group can
    identify which person is depicted in which part of each poster!

10 **Take some instant photos.** Obtain an instamatic camera and, as partici-
    pants arrive, with permission, take their photos. Display the photos
    around the wall, with a blank sheet of paper alongside each. Then ask
    each person to write up one positive feature they can identify through
    the photos of at least one other person. As the course progresses, ask
    participants to write further good points alongside photos as appropri-
    ate (but only *good* points).

13

Gathering and using expectations

As trainers we sometimes feel we have to give participants what we know they need. However, we should never do this at the expense of missing an opportunity to find out what they *want* – and making the most of common ground between their needs and wishes.

1 **Make your own provisional agenda clear first.** Show participants the intended outcomes of the training event, and say a few words about how you plan to go about achieving these outcomes. Make it clear, however, that you are about to enter in to fine-tuning to meet participants' expectations.

2 **Ask participants, 'What do you personally most wish to get out of this programme?'** Give them time to think, and don't ask them for verbal replies – the first few replies could divert the ideas of participants who are slower to reply. It's best to get them to write their expectations down. This can be done by giving everyone a small piece of acetate (a quarter of an A4 sheet is usually enough) and an overhead projector pen. Ask them to add their names to their expectations (this helps you keep track of who is wanting what).

3 **If necessary, put participants into small groups to discuss and decide their expectations.** This can be useful if you sense that there are several participants who don't really have any clear expectations yet. 'Group expectations' are also useful if you've got more than, say, 24 participants, when it could be too time-consuming to look at all their individual expectations.

4 **Share their expectations in plenary session.** Put their acetate slips in turn on the overhead projector. Invite particular participants to clarify or expand on any expectations that seem to need this. Seeing their own handwriting up on the screen helps participants to feel a sense of ownership of the fine-tuning you are making to your training event.

5 **Show their expectations in random order.** This is better than collecting them in the order that participants happen to be sitting and then showing them in this order. Random order helps keep participants' attention focused – at least until their own acetates have been shown.

6 **If useful, let participants introduce themselves briefly while their expectations are on-screen.** This is useful if they don't already know each other, and can save the time of having a purely-introductions round. You can keep introductions to a reasonable time when necessary by removing one acetate and pressing on with the next!

7 **Keep your replies to their expectations brief.** It's useful to say now and then 'Yes, we'll certainly be dealing with this later in today's programme', but don't make a detailed argument concerning why you're *not* intending to address particular expectations.

8 **Keep the expectations in common view.** This is easily done by gently pasting the backs of the acetate slips with a glue stick, and sticking them lightly on a flipchart. This helps participants feel that you are taking their expectations seriously.

9 **Return to particular expectations as your training event develops.** Link things you intended to do anyway to particular requests from participants – give them the credit of thinking of sensible issues to address!

10 **Return to the expectations towards the close of your training event.** If the acetate slips have been pasted lightly enough, you can remove them from the flipchart again and display them once more, asking whether each participant is satisfied.

14

Harnessing the 'want' to learn

When people really want to learn something, it should not surprise us how successful they are in their learning. The more you can create or amplify your participants' want to learn, the more productive will be your training events.

1 **Make your advance publicity attractive.** If the intended training outcomes look relevant and clear, and if the planned training event processes look well-organized and contain variety, your participants should arrive with a healthy 'want' to learn.

2 **Be likeable!** First impressions count a lot. If your participants like you, they will be much more likely to want to learn from you. Smiles go a long way. Also, don't create tension by showing any frustration you feel – for example, when a participant arrives late.

3 **Find out what participants already want.** We've included a set of tips on identifying and harnessing participants' expectations elsewhere. When you know what they want, give them as much as you can of it – as well as other things you know they need!

4 **Remember to address the question, 'Why?'** When participants are trying to master something new, they need to have good reasons for making an effort.

5 **Work out 'What's in it for you is. . .'.** Sometimes, a training programme is naturally geared to the needs of the company or organization; however, it always helps to identify benefits of becoming trained that relate to your individual participants. One way of approaching this is to ask them outright: 'What's in it for you?' and to help them add each other's answers to their own.

6 **Value participants' existing skills and knowledge.** Where possible, avoid telling them things they already know! Give *them* the credit for contributing ideas and information. When participants feel valued, they want to learn more.

7 **Make it *their* training event, not yours.** Use their words on flipcharted summaries of discussions. Stick up the products of *their* groupwork for all to see.

8 **Give participants choices.** For example, let them choose whether to do a task individually or in small groups – be prepared to let some work individually while others choose to work collaboratively. When possible, give a short menu of tasks that individuals and groups can choose from.

9 **Be prepared to negotiate.** For example, in a residential course, an unplanned 'swimming or siesta' afternoon may be repaid amply by participants' increased productivity later in the course.

10 **Be enthusiastic – but not threateningly so.** Enthusiasm is infectious, and can amplify the want to learn – as long as participants don't feel intimidated by your zeal.

15

Following-up pre-event tasks

There is nothing worse for participants than having done some preparation for a training event, only to find that what they did is never mentioned again! Here are some ways of ensuring that the efforts participants put in to preparing for your training events are recognized, valued and used.

1 **Don't forget what you asked participants to do before attending.** Keep the exact wording of your pre-event tasks in sight.

2 **Ask participants for any problems they encountered in the tasks.** If they have not attempted them, they will be very quiet at this stage. However, those participants who did have a go at them will have their chance to bring any problems to the surface, and will feel pleased to be able to do so.

3 **Where possible, set tasks so that participants can bring their 'product' along to your training event.** It will be clear that some participants have tried the task and that others have not. It is useful then to put participants into small groups, asking them to summarize their products for discussion at the next plenary session.

4 **Don't leave any pre-event task cold.** Anyone who has invested time and effort into having a go at such a task will feel devalued if you never refer to the task again. Make sure that all pre-event tasks are built into your programme in one way or another.

5 **Give participants time to catch up on what they should have done!** For all sorts of reasons, some participants will not have attempted your pre-event tasks, or will not even have received the instructions. Allow short but reasonable amounts of time for participants individually (or in groups) to make up for what they have not yet attempted.

6   **Have some examples to hand.** It can often be useful to show partici-
    pants at your training events the sorts of things that past participants
    did with your pre-event tasks. Sometimes, the main message will be
    how much better your present participants have tackled the tasks than
    anyone has ever done before – this makes for happy training events!

7   **'Here is one I cooked earlier.'** Your own answer to a pre-event task is
    particularly useful when you know it will be (or already has been) sur-
    passed by the work of your participants. Conversely, resist the
    temptation to show them the one you 'cooked earlier' when their work
    is not up to the standard you expected.

8   **Consider setting a choice of tasks.** This can allow different participants
    to have attempted different things – helping you to make the most of
    the possibilities of them giving feedback to each other.

9   **Ask participants, 'What pre-event tasks should I set next time?'** You
    will usually find that you learn a lot from this, and can use it next time
    to advantage!

10 **Monitor the outcomes of pre-event tasks.** The main benefit you can
    derive may be simply to adjust the wording of the task instructions
    ready for next time, so that you can confidently expect everyone to try
    to do what you really want them to try to do.

16

Designing performance criteria for participants' work

Nowadays, learning outcomes are increasingly being expressed in terms of the things people will be able to do when they have achieved the targets of training programmes. In particular, participants at your training events will need to be able to tell for themselves whether they have attained suitable levels of performance. The following suggestions may help you to share the intended outcomes with participants.

1 **Remember that performance is about competence; knowledge is only a means to this end.** Remind your participants that it's one thing to know how to do something, but another thing to be able to do it really well.

2 **Express your training event aims and objectives in terms of performance.** Make them into a clear agenda of what participants are expected to be able to deliver themselves when they have completed their training programme.

3 **Specify the evidence.** The best way to help participants at your training events to see exactly what they are intended to become able to achieve is to give them clear examples of 'what it will look like' when they achieve the aims and objectives of the programme.

4 **Invite further aims and objectives.** Different participants will rightly have their own interpretation of what they need to become able to do, and how they can demonstrate that they have achieved their own objectives.

5 **Let participants help you to translate aims and objectives to their real world.** As trainers, we often have an overall view of what we want our participants to achieve – but their own view of how their achievements need to relate to their own particular work environments is even more useful and important.

6 **Ensure that performance criteria are realistic and measurable.** It is all too easy to become trapped in rhetoric. Keep performance criteria to the realities – avoid the intangibles!

7 **Use 'What this really means is. . .'.** Often, performance criteria and outcomes can be too vague. Sharing with participants the practical realities is always a positive forward step.

8 **Let participants put the outcomes in their own words.** This can help to give them the feeling of ownership of the skills and abilities you are trying to help them to achieve and develop.

9 **Measure the outcomes.** This means devising tasks and activities which enable you and your participants to find out how well (or otherwise) your participants are progressing towards achieving the aims of your training programmes.

10 **Research how much your participants feel they have advanced.** This means finding out what they believe they can now do as a result of participating in your training events, and also what they believe they can't yet do.

17

Making a learning contract

One way of transferring the ownership of a training event to the participants is to involve them in making a learning contract. Here are some ideas on how you can pass over this control to them.

1 **Provide a selection of objectives.** Then ask participants to 'vote' on them, for example by giving their first choice five stars, second choice four stars and so on. Then collect up the numbers of stars for each objective, and arrange the objectives in participants' order of priority.

2 **Work out new objectives.** Ask participants what they particularly wish to achieve during the training event, and formulate additional (or replacement) objectives for the session.

3 **Establish some ground rules.** Having identified the proposed content of the training event, invite participants to suggest some rules for how the event should proceed. Suggest that they formulate rules regarding their own contributions, as well as rules regarding the contribution you are expected to make.

4 **Establish ownership of objectives.** Provide a list of all the possible objectives of the session, and ask participants to identify which objectives they personally are keen to achieve. Get them to write their names alongside such objectives on a flipchart or overhead.

5 **Ask participants, 'What do you want me to do?'** It is often really useful to clarify what they expect of their training event facilitator, and what they expect to be able to handle under their own steam.

6 **Decide on the evidence that will correspond to 'success'.** Ask participants what they consider will be the evidence that they have achieved their objectives from the training event, and how it will be possible for them to decide that they have been successful.

7 **Decide roles.** Help participants to work out *how* they will work together to achieve the objectives that have been identified in the learning contract. Help participants to decide who will do what on the way. Also work out the criteria for success. Help participants to see what evidence will constitute demonstrable proof that they have achieved their objectives.

8 **Use the Internet.** Ask participants to think of a message that they would like to receive on the Internet, describing what the session is all about and what they have achieved.

9 **Paint a picture.** Ask participants, in small groups, to produce a picture depicting the scene that they hope will have occurred by the end of the session – but without using any words. Give each group a maximum of one minute to explain their picture to the rest of the participants.

10 **Create a concertina letter.** Let participants sort themselves into small groups. Give each group one piece of paper. Ask person number 1 in each group to write down one thing that they hope to be able to say to their managers, regarding things they will be able to do as a result of the training event. Then ask person 1 in each group to fold down their statements so that successive members of the group can't see them as they in turn write down their own statements. Then unfold the 'concertinaed' sheets and display them on walls, or ask a member from each group to read out the whole list. Revisit the lists towards the close of the session, asking if anyone wants to change or add anything. Encourage people to talk to their actual managers about things in 'the letter'.

18

Brainstorming

'Brainstorming' should be a quick way of gaining a lot of ideas, without any restrictions on validity of the ideas that may emerge. Here are some suggested ways of ensuring that brainstorming sessions work well and productively.

1 **Suggest that all ideas are welcome.** One of the fundamental principles of brainstorming is 'free thought' and it is important in the early phases that no ideas are subject to criticism or rebuke.

2 **Allow anyone to 'pass'.** It is important that participants feel that if at the time they have no new ideas to offer, they are not regarded as inferior.

3 **Get participants to write their ideas on post-its.** Their post-its can subsequently be stuck to a flipchart (or wall) in any order, and the order rearranged as the shape of the general flow of ideas emerges.

4 **Use small bits of overhead transparency for brainstorming now and then.** The advantage of this is that participants' own words, in their own handwriting, can appear for all to see on the screen. This can be time-saving compared to writing up their words on a flipchart.

5 **Sometimes, put participants into groups to brainstorm.** This is particularly useful when you know that some participants are new to the area to be explored, and may not have particular experience to offer. Ask the groups to prioritize the suggestions which emerge in their discussions.

6 **Continue till there are no more new ideas.** Sometimes, you may feel that all the useful ideas have already been contributed, but it is important to wait until all your participants have had their say. This is a way of giving them ownership over the whole range of ideas which will be subsequently explored and developed.

7   **Establish participants' view of the relative importance of ideas.** For example, number the principal ideas, say, from one to twelve, ask them to 'vote' for the six most important ideas on the list, and record their votes alongside each idea.

8   **Invite any further ideas.** Often, after a brainstorm, participants may be able to think of further ideas (or better ideas) that have not already surfaced.

9   **Ask, 'How should we best approach this idea?' in turn.** This helps to establish participants' ownership over the processes whereby your training event will address each item on the agenda that they have identified.

10 **Keep the products of brainstorms in view.** For example, stick up flipcharts on the walls. Show that you value the results of brainstorming sessions by referring to these flipcharts when appropriate as the training event progresses, and remember that it is never too late to add further ideas to flipcharts produced earlier.

Chapter 3 Using Things Around You

Our suggestions in this chapter are mainly about training resources and the training environment. We start by looking at the importance of the accommodation that participants themselves will use during training sessions, and the effect of this environment on how they feel and how they perform during the sessions.

Most training rooms are equipped with overhead projectors, and most trainers now use these on a regular basis. However, familiarity with the overhead projector can blind us to some of the ways in which we fail to exploit them really well. Next time you go to a large conference, take particular note of how different presenters use (or make bad use of) overhead projectors – we can all learn just as much from bad practice as good practice! We offer some suggestions based on our experience of trying to use overhead projectors effectively.

Another common training aid is the flipchart. Again, there are things that can all too easily go wrong with the use of flipcharts, and we offer some suggestions regarding making their use more effective, and also making it less time-consuming.

The chalkboard or blackboard was once the most common medium in the training room, but nowadays these have been largely replaced by markerboards or whiteboards. We offer some straightforward suggestions for avoiding some of the problems that can beset the use of these media.

Years ago, trainees spent a lot of training sessions just writing down things that their trainers said, and copying down things that trainers wrote up on boards. Life is too short for that! It is much easier now to package up the content of a training programme into handouts, or learning packages, or manuals, and spend the actual training sessions *doing things* with the information, rather than just having trainees copy it out. Our suggestions on the design and use of handouts are intended to help make the task of deciding what to package up in this way easier.

With the ready availability of a rapidly expanding (and already vast) range of training video materials, it is more and more common to have a video playback machine and monitor (or several monitors) in a well-equipped training room. Most of us also have similar machines at home. We offer not ten but twenty tips regarding the use of video in training sessions. We look not only at getting the machinery to work the way we want it, and when we need it, we also look at some factors relating to *why* we may choose to use video in training sessions, and *how* we can really integrate it into the fabric of training programmes. One of the problems with television is that we are quite conditioned to sit back and relax and let it go over our heads – not ideal if there is a significant training message we wish to be captured by our participants!

19

Seating, tables and work-space

Participants can become very bored if they are always sitting in the same chair in the same place and with the same neighbours – even in a training event lasting just a day, let alone an extended residential course!

1 **Try to find rooms which lend themselves to variety.** Training rooms where chairs and tables can be moved around easily are best. Tiered lecture theatres and boardrooms with heavy tables are worst!

2 **Don't encourage participants to hide behind tables.** When there is a table between them and you, it is somehow easier for them to sit passively and lean on the table – even fall asleep. With nothing to lean on, people are more attentive and involved. Having tables scattered around the edge of the room is better.

3 **Be kind to bums!** Use your own experience to decide what sorts of chairs are best. Remember that participants will be sitting down for longer periods than you will. Concentration spans are less to do with brains, and more to do with bums!

4 **Don't have too many chairs.** Have only two or three spare chairs; stack up any others in a secluded corner or, better still, get them out of the room altogether. Spare chairs often become a no-go zone near the trainer (people sit at the back if there's a back to sit at). Alternatively, spare chairs get occupied by coats, bags or briefcases.

5 **Avoid straight lines or rows of chairs.** A circle of chairs, or a U-shape, works better for an introductory plenary session (with any tables behind the chairs). Try to arrange the chairs so that all participants have an uninterrupted view of you, and of the projector screen and flipchart. Don't be afraid to move chairs!

6 **Help ensure that participants can see each others' faces.** Again, circles and U-shapes work best. When participants can observe each other easily, they get to know each other better and more quickly, and feel more involved in your training event right from the start.

7 **Have no safe hiding place!** Have you noticed that in rectangular table layouts, the most awkward participants always seem to establish themselves in one or other of the back corners? If there aren't any corners to start with, this can't happen. However, when you set out your circle or U-shape, make sure that there are no chairs anywhere near any tables that are in the back corners!

8 **Weigh up the need for notetaking in plenaries.** Decide whether to use handout materials to save participants having to passively copy things down, or whether the act of making notes will help them to remember the material in their own ways.

9 **Now find a table!** When you give participants individual or group tasks to do, invite them to move their chairs to any of the tables round the edge of the room (and not the tables to their chairs). This also helps you to be able to circulate freely, and speak to them in groups or individually as necessary.

10 **Make full use of any other rooms you have available.** Having additional rooms for syndicate work gives participants a change. Make sure that the same syndicate isn't stuck in the same syndicate room for session after session – ring the changes and give everyone some variety. Move the plenary location around too if there is more than one room big enough.

20

Using overhead projectors

Probably the most common device at our disposal in our training sessions is the overhead projector. Making good use of projectors can make all the difference between a professionally run training event and a shambles. The following suggestions may help you get the most out of your OHP.

1   **Know your machine.** If you're working on home ground, this is not an issue. However, if you're working in a new training room, it's well worth your time to take steps to become familiar with the particular machine you're going to work with. Don't be afraid to move it to get it into good focus.

2   **Get the position right.** The aim is to ensure that all your participants can see the screen without anything obstructing their vision (particularly *you*!) Put on a slide and sit in various seats in the room (before the participants are there) so that you know that the screen is clearly visible, and that the average overhead will be easily seen.

3   **Be ready for problems!** If the bulb should suddenly go, is there a 'switchable' spare? Check that this works. Alternatively, have a spare projector (which you know works) sitting inconspicuously in a corner of the room – or in the boot of your car!

4   **When all else fails. . . .** Have one or two exercises up your sleeve which do not depend at all on the availability of an overhead projector. Plan these so that while your participants are engaged on them, you give yourself the time to arrange a new projector.

5   **Use the top half of the screen.** By sliding your transparencies 'up', you can normally make the most important pieces of information appear towards the top of the screen – more easily visible by participants at your sessions.

6   **Don't use typewritten overheads.** To be clearly visible, most fonts need to be of '18', '24' or even '36' size – considerably bigger and bolder than typical typewritten materials.

7 **Keep the words down.** A good overhead transparency only needs to contain the main ideas, not the details. You can add the details as you discuss the main points on the transparencies. Your own 'crib' notes can then be written onto your paper copy.

8 **'The medium is the message'.** Good-quality overheads can add credibility to your messages. It's worth using desk-top-publishing programmes to make your principal overhead transparencies look professional and believable. A really important event may warrant coloured transparencies with graphics.

9 **Remember to switch the thing off!** Most overhead projectors make at least some noise. When you're not actually showing something, it's important that both visually and auditorily you are not distracting your participants.

10 **Give people time to take notes if they wish.** Sometimes, you may have copies of your transparencies in handout materials you issue to participants. Otherwise, expect that at least some participants will want to jot down the main points they see on the screen, and make sure that they've done this before you move on to another transparency.

21

Using flipcharts

After the overhead projector, flipcharts are probably the most common of visual media used by trainers. The following suggestions may help you make your use of this medium professional and trouble-free.

1 **Set it up before you start.** Some flipchart stands have a will of their own, and seem to come provided with three legs of unequal length. Don't let your participants see you struggle with the thing!

2 **Bring your own pens.** There's nothing more frustrating than a flipchart without proper pens. Overhead projector pens will do in a crisis, but your lettering will look spidery and may be hard to read at the back of the room.

3 **Don't put too much on a flipchart.** It's best to 'write big' and use broad pens, so that everyone can see all the words without difficulty. Unless your handwriting is unusually good (neither of ours is!) you may find it best to print capital letters when writing on flipcharts. But remember, too many capital letters tend to generate eye fatigue.

4 **Don't forget your Blu-tack.** You may often want to display several flipcharts at the same time, so make sure you've got that essential means of sticking flipcharts to doors, walls and even windows. Be careful, however, if walls are wallpapered – it's still possible to stick flipcharts to such walls as long as you develop the knack of using Blu-tack sparingly, and gently peel off the chart with the Blu-tack still sticking to the chart rather than to the wallpaper.

5 **Make it easy to tear off successive flipcharts.** With pads of perforated flipchart paper, this is straightforward. However, usually you will have to make your own arrangements for removing sheets. Often, it helps to simply unscrew the two knobs which secure the chart to the easel, allowing you to make clean, neat tear-offs at the very top of the pad of charts.

6 **A sharp knife can be useful.** For example, there are small collapsible razor-knives. With these, you can (with practice) score along the top of a chart neatly and tear it off leaving a straight edge at the top. Be careful not to cut more than one sheet at a time though!

7 **Decide when 'live' flipcharting really is a sensible choice.** Don't end up writing long sentences dictated by participants. Flipcharts work best for keywords, for example in brainstorming sessions.

8 **Prepare important flipcharts in advance.** For example, if you're going to use flipcharts to write up tasks for participants to do in your training event, it's useful to be able to turn straight to a ready-made flipchart rather than write it all out with them watching.

9 **Get participants to use flipcharts.** For example, giving a syndicate a flipchart as a means of reporting-back on the task they are doing can help concentrate their minds on the task in hand, rather than engaging in sophisticated work-avoidance strategies!

10 **Always have some rubber bands.** Often, you'll want to take away the flipcharts produced at a training event, so you can write up a report on the event, or collate and distribute the products of the event. An armful of loose flipcharts is not an easy package to carry away – but rolled up tightly with a couple of rubber bands, they're much more manageable.

22

Using markerboards/ chalkboards

It's often assumed that anyone can use these things well. One thing is often forgotten – why use them? To use them wisely, there has to be an intended learning payoff for participants. The following ideas combine good reasons for using such visual aids with techniques for using them professionally.

1   **Have a clear purpose in mind.** For example, participants may be expected to note down what you write, or the visual display may be intended to be there for a while to provide focus for subsequent participant activity and discussion.

2   **Don't write too small.** Your writing needs to be visible from the furthest point in the room – this determines the minimum size of your writing on markerboards or chalkboards.

3   **Consider other ways of disseminating information.** It is often better to issue a handout containing information than to write it up yourself for participants to note down. The use of markerboards or chalkboards is probably best restricted to things that emerge during a session, rather than the basic information on which the session is based.

4   **Use markerboards/chalkboards to capture matters arising.** When ideas emerge during a session, 'get them on the wall' where they can safely reside until such time as they can be adequately dealt with. This is particularly useful for defusing confrontational situations, and is much better than trying to pretend that there is no cause to debate the matters arising.

5   **Normal handwriting is usually not suitable.** Unless you have a (fast) naturally attractive script, it's probably better to use capital letters than 'joined-up writing' when using chalkboards or markerboards. Ordinary script on prepared overheads may indeed be easier to read than capitals, but the same does not seem to apply to handwriting on boards.

6 **Use 'bullet-points' rather than whole sentences.** The time it takes to write long sentences can be irritating to participants, especially if they're also trying to note the sentences down themselves.

7 **Squeaky chalk is painful!** Most of us remember this from our school-days. Breaking a stick of chalk in two usually yields a chalk surface which writes more freely.

8 **On markerboards, use the right pens!** Pens need to be non-permanent and erasable! Also, the thickness of the pens needs to be appropriate for the size of the room and the maximum distance from participants' positions.

9 **Use colours wisely.** A single colour soon becomes monotonous. Separate colours can help different points to stand out from a list. Colour can be used to prioritize and to show what's really important.

10 **Don't erase too soon.** Participants can feel manipulated if you remove information from their view before they've had the chance to note it down themselves, or at least complete their thinking about it.

23

Designing and using handouts

Handout materials are often very important in terms of participants' learning from a training event. It is these materials that participants can refer to again and again, at their own pace. Such materials can also help you make best use of the face-to-face opportunities that a training event provides.

1 **Plan to use handouts to save having to tell participants things.** Some participants may already know them. It's much quicker for everyone to scan a handout than to listen to you explaining everything in person.When part of your training event is intended to tell participants things, see how much you can put into handout materials.

2 **Make sure you have sufficient copies.** There are often a couple of unexpected participants – and some may want to have an extra copy to give to an absent colleague. It pays to be ready to give anyone or everyone copies of anything that is relevant to the aims or objectives of your training event.

3 **Make handouts look attractive.** Use desk-top-publishing software to give your handouts that look of professionalism and style. The medium is the message – scrappy handouts (however good their content) will devalue your messages. Graphics can also help to make your handouts look better and more memorable.

4 **Make handouts interactive.** Build in tasks and activities, so that anyone looking again at your handouts can relive the experience of being at your training event. The most important dimension is what participants may do when trying the tasks and activities you build into your handout materials.

5 **Use handout material in advance.** Send participants handouts containing the things that your training event is going to be based upon, so that when they arrive to participate in your training events they are all at a similar level of knowledge or expertise.

6   **Include space for participants to make the handouts their own.** When participants write their own comments, reactions, or answers to questions onto their own copies of the handout materials, they immediately gain a sense of ownership of the materials. They are no longer just pieces of paper they were given during a training event.

7   **Specify the aims and objectives of your training events on handouts.** This helps participants to link your agenda to theirs, and to know exactly what the purpose of your training events may be.

8   **Include 'Further Reading' lists in handouts.** There's nothing better than an 'Annotated Bibliography'. Give your own comments to help participants to know what they should aim to extract from the sources you list.

9   **Put your handout materials onto computer disk.** Any and every handout benefits from the experience you gain each time you use it. When your materials are on disk, you can continually update and improve them.

10 **Include a 'feedback sheet' in your handouts.** A simple questionnaire can give you a range of ideas to incorporate into the next issue of each handout. Don't forget to ask 'what's missing?' from any edition of a handout.

24
Using video machines and tapes

It's normally possible to arrange for a video player and monitor to be available at a training event; many training rooms have such things as standard equipment. The following suggestions may help you (and your participants) get the most from video.

1 **Arrive early.** You may think you know everything there is to know about video players, but this location will certainly have a different one. And you'll need to find who went off after the last session with the remote control in their pocket.

2 **Know your machine!** One video player looks much like another, but they all have their ways. A couple of minutes trying to get it to start can seem like an hour with all eyes on our efforts! Get a certificate in video handling! Why can't manufacturers standardize all those machines? Try and practise on as many different machines as you can – or ensure that there is a 6-year-old in your group who will quickly make any machine do anything you want.

3 **Make friends with the local technician!** Suddenly you will realize that you need an extension lead, or the machine is locked up, or the colour or sound will go off for no reason, or the machine won't start at all. 'I've got a problem, I'm afraid, and I'd be really grateful if you could help me out' is a much better opening sentence than, 'Are you the person in charge of this bloody video?'

4 **Arrange suitable weather, or check the blackout facilities.** It is really frustrating being a member of the audience with the sun shining in your eyes or on the screen. Work out where the sun will be when you plan to show your video. If no blackout facilities are available and it's the middle of summer, you may need to be flexible and reschedule your video for when the sun has moved round a bit!

5 **Check visibility.** Before the training event or during a break, check whether the most distant participants will still have a reasonable view of the television set. Try to place the set on a high table if participants' heads may obscure the view of those sitting further back. If necessary, rearrange the chairs for the slot where you're going to use video.

6 **Time your showing.** Try not to guess how long the interview on tape lasts. Time it and tell your participants. You may be able to play a really good video that lasts 30 minutes, but it does help participants' 'mind-set' to know how long they will have to sit and watch it. Don't be afraid to stop and start the tape and allow discussion in between – watch participants' body language for signs of boredom.

7 **Check that the security tab has been removed.** This stops the children, the next-door neighbour or the technician recording 'Top of the Pops' or 'Match of the Day' over your £600 video tape.

8 **Check the 'X' rating.** Do make sure that you bring the correct tape along and that the children have not put the wrong cover on it – or the wrong label. Particularly make sure that it's not something that came from the back room of the video hire shop! Check for potential offence. Even innocuous training videos can contain things which can offend people. Apply your equal opportunities checklist to the video. Watch for bad language, gender or racial inequality, all of which can easily offend.

9 **Know the content of your videotape.** It's easy to think that just because you saw the tape last year, you can remember everything on it. Try and view it a couple of times before the event, making notes. You could find this really useful if you arrive at the venue to find there's not a remote control, or the number-counter measures metres of tape rather than minutes! Then you'll be depending on your memory as you fast-forward or back. Now, did that interview with Daxa come before or after the view of the castle. . . !

10 **Fix an electronic tab to your tape that bleeps if you leave it behind.** In your haste to get away at the end of an event it's easy to leave the tape behind. Also if you forget to take it out of the machine after you've shown it, it's not very easy to see. One of us was ten miles out of town before realizing that the video still in the machine had been promised to someone else for use next day.

11 **Plan an alternative!** The best laid plans of mice and humans gang oft agley (Burns, after applying equal ops). It can be really embarrassing after you've geared up your group to watch this really important video only to find it does not work – and yes, you did arrive early, and it was working then! Just have one or two alternatives up your sleeve.

12 **Are you getting past it?** A favourite video that you used often and to great effect five years ago may have been really good then, but could be quite dated now. When you watch an old video carefully, you may be surprised how fast times change. If the video looks 'dated', your whole message could be undermined.

13 **Have the tape at the right place to start.** If you're trying to locate a particular part of a programme using fast-forward and fast-reverse while everyone watches and waits, you may find that you simply can't find the bit you want at all!

14 **Remember people's attitudes to television.** We're conditioned to forget quite quickly most of what we see on our small screens. We're also conditioned to use television as a medium for relaxation rather than a learning resource. If you want television to serve a useful learning function during your training events, you will need to overcome such conditioning.

15 **Have a definite purpose for using video.** Work out exactly what you intend your participants to gain from viewing a video, and make the aims clear to them before you use the programme. Where possible, use video to help participants achieve things they could not have achieved using any other medium. For example, video can help to bring to the forefront such dimensions as body language, tone of voice and facial expression – all of which can be more powerful than printed words.

16 **Remember that concentration spans are short.** It is often better to plan to use a few selected clips than to try to show a programme lasting half-an-hour. The most useful control on the video machine is the pause button!

17 **Prepare an agenda in advance.** With participants, if possible, make a list of questions or issues which you wish to gain information on by means of the video. Where participants are watching a video with some definite intentions, there is much more chance that their watching will be attentive.

18 **Follow each clip by a discussion session.** Help participants to reflect on what they've learned from the video – or to use ideas from the video to promote deeper debates.

19 **Keep the video available.** Some participants may want to have another look at things they've seen, and it may be possible for them to do this in breaks in your programme.

20 **Remember to collect feedback on the usefulness (or otherwise) of the video.** Include questions about the video in your evaluation questionnaire.

Chapter 4 Keeping Your Training Events Going

This chapter is mainly about training event processes, though we have anticipated our discussion of many of these already in this book. We start by reflecting on the importance of active learning, and designing training events around what participants will actually *do* rather than around things we may tell them!

We thought it worth bringing into this discussion some suggestions for 'avoiding alienation' – in other words keeping all participants pulling together as best we can.

Probably a hallmark of experienced and successful trainers is the way such people seem to handle the unexpected without flapping or fretting. For new trainers, meeting the unexpected can be a nightmare situation! The more confident you become as a trainer, the more you will actually enjoy the challenge of taking on the unexpected – and you may even go out looking for it. We hope our suggestions will help.

Next, we offer a range of ideas intended to help develop participants' creativity. Creative problem solving is a very useful skill, both in the world of work and in everyday life, and we find that participants often warm to an element of creativity during training events.

Next we move to the important area of 'working one-to-one' with individual participants. For the participants themselves, this can often be both the most valuable – but the most stressful – part of a training programme. We hope that our suggestions will help you to maximize the benefits and minimize the risks.

Training events provide opportunities for participants to learn a great deal from feedback they receive from each other as well as from their train-ers. We provide suggestions to help you to build in as much learning from feedback as possible, and to structure it in ways where the feedback will be readily received.

Making sense of what we learn is something that often happens some considerable time after we learned it! We provide some suggestions that may help your participants reflect on what they're learning during your sessions, and therefore gain a deeper feel for what they do in your training events.

You'll gather from our title, 'Presentations – if you must!' that neither of us is keen on formal presentations. We like *giving* them well enough, but we hate sitting listening to them, so we reckon that most people don't really learn much by sitting listening!

Much of the real learning at good training events happens when partici-pants work in syndicates or groups. It also helps to take the pressure off individuals who may be feeling apprehensive. Our next two sets of sugges-tions refer respectively to syndicates where participants normally have definite tasks to perform, and 'home groups' where the group may be given considerable freedom in how it approaches its work. We next take a look at the benefits which can be achieved by using role plays.

The part of a training event which naturally remains freshest in partici-pants' minds is the very end. If a session ends badly, participants will tend to spread that feeling to their impression of the whole event. If it ends really positively, they will leave wearing rose-coloured spectacles. It's worth planning for a good conclusion (and not a rushed one), so we've put some suggestions under the heading 'End with a bang!'

25

Maximize 'learning-by-doing'

Most people learn far more by having a go at things themselves than by listening to someone who can already do them. Make your training events active learning experiences.

1 **Remind participants how they really learn.** Ask them to think of something they know that they are good at (but not to write it down). Then ask them to write down *how* they became good at whatever it was – post-it slips are suitable for this. Then point out to them how most of their successful learning has been by practising, having a go, and so on.

2 **Value 'getting things wrong' as a way of learning.** When our participants feel there is no shame in making mistakes, they will be more willing to try anything – and they will be more tolerant of our own mistakes! It's worth reminding participants that there should be no such thing as 'failure', only feedback.

3 **Plan your training events around things for participants to do.** These ingredients are more important than things you wish to tell them. A successful training event is often a series of participant activities, linked together by very small briefing and discussion episodes.

4 **Make the task instructions clear and simple.** If everyone – trainers and participants – knows exactly what they are trying to do, there is much more chance that they will do it well. It can be a great help to have tasks written down on overhead transparencies, so everyone can see them clearly and, if necessary, for long enough to really understand them.

5 **Be ready to negotiate tasks.** Where the task you had planned turns out to be not entirely relevant to participants' needs or expectations, be prepared to adjust the task briefing with their help to make it more suitable.

6   **Give participants time.** While it is good practice to set a time limit for each task, use your eyes and ears to discover whether participants have sufficient time. If they are given too much time they can become impatient to press on. If they are in the middle of a useful learning experience when 'time is up', it is well worth extending the deadline.

7   **Value the things participants do.** Even when they get things wrong, don't make them feel their efforts were in vain. Celebrate their successes when they do things correctly or well.

8   **Have a go at your own tasks!** 'Here is one I prepared earlier' is not the same as having a fresh attempt at a task. Even better, extol how much better your participants' attempts are than the one you've just made.

9   **Provide escape routes.** When you are using a task that will be very difficult for some participants, think of using the option to work in groups rather than individually. Alternatively, think of some tasks that are more straightforward to set those who have not the experience to attempt the hard ones.

10 **Let participants set *you* tasks.** Show that you yourself are willing to have a go at things you've not tried to do before. Better still, let participants tell you how you could have gone about it more successfully!

26

Avoiding alienation

People are all different, but they don't like being made to *feel* different. The following suggestions show some ways of avoiding turning particular participants into deadly enemies!

1   **Get to know all names, not just some.** It's almost like an insult when someone doesn't know your name, but knows other people's names. Using place cards, or (large) lapel badges helps you to get to know names in a group, and also helps the group members to get to know each other.

2   **Get names right!** If you call someone by the wrong name, or spell names incorrectly, you risk making enemies, or at least losing friends! There's no better way of checking the spelling of people's names than getting them to write their own names on place cards or badges. That way, you'll find out whether Jonathan prefers to be called Jon (and not John), and whether Victoria prefers to be called Vikki – or Vicky.

3   **Avoid racism.** Even with a group of the same ethnic origin, some people will be sensitive to even the slightest hint of prejudice. With multiracial groups, be particularly careful to treat every member equally. This includes making it your business to be able to pronounce unusual names correctly – 'How exactly do I pronounce your name?' is a useful way of showing you care about equality.

4   **Avoid sexism.** This is particularly important with mixed groups of course. The main offending words tend to be 'he', 'his', 'him', especially when talking of situations that are equally applicable to women as to men. 'S/he' is clumsy and unsatisfactory. 'He or she' only draws attention to the issue. Plurals are usually much safer – there are few problems with 'they', 'them' and 'their'.

5   **Treat people equally.** You can't be expected to 'like' all participants equally, but you can take positive steps not to pick on anyone you like least, and not to appear to 'warm to' anyone you like more.

6 **Avoid taking sides.** When there is a split of opinion within a group –
   even when you're definitely on one side – try to be seen to be reflecting
   the opposing arguments and viewpoints fairly and objectively, rather
   than ganging up with the people whose ideas coincide with your own.

7 **No one likes a loser.** If things turn out against you – no coffee, no
   handouts, no heat, too much noise. . . the list is endless – don't go on
   and on about how you tried to arrange it all and it isn't your fault.
   Accept the adversity on behalf of the whole group, and look for productive ways forward which minimize the inconvenience. Above all,
   don't publicly blame the person whose 'fault' it is – do this privately
   later!

8 **Don't set yourself apart.** If you are 'apart' – for example, very distin-
   guished in your field – they'll know this already! Avoid
   'name-dropping' and other temptations. It's also well worth avoiding
   unnecessary jargon in your sessions.

9 **Don't queue-jump.** We all know how it feels when an 'important person' slips ahead in the queue for lunch! It's better to suffice with eating
   the leftovers from the buffet than to alienate your participants by being
   seen to be exercising special privileges.

10 **Avoid 'top tables'.** This particularly applies to residential training
   events lasting several days. However much you feel you need to be
   talking to the client over lunch or dinner, it counts a lot if you are seen
   to be mixing with your participants. Besides, they tend to be much better company!

27

Coping with the unexpected

Your reputation as a trainer will depend not only on your professional expertise, but on your ability to be seen to cope with the unexpected, calmly, professionally, and with humour and dignity. The following suggestions may help you to attain this image.

1 **Welcome the unexpected!** Life is full of the unexpected. It is only an enemy if we resist it. Look at it this way: a 'competent' trainer works within what is expected; a 'professional' trainer can work within whatever turns up. Aim to be able to cope with anything. Don't worry that you don't succeed every time – no one can.

2 **Harness the unexpected.** Work out what it really means. Define it. Put it into words which everyone shares the meaning of.

3 **Turn the unexpected into 'issues' and 'questions'.** Add these to the questions and issues upon which your training event is based. Sometimes, the things that arise from unexpected developments are more important than the original issues or questions that your training event was meant to address.

4 **Seek everyone's views.** When the unexpected turns up, don't feel that you are obliged to have all the answers up your sleeve. It can be the ideal opportunity to say, 'I don't really know – what do you think?' to your participants. They will respect you all the more for this.

5 **Legitimize the unexpected.** When important matters turn up 'unexpectedly', add these formally to the agenda of your training session. Turn them into additional objectives or intended outcomes.

6 **Ask for the unexpected.** Keep asking, 'What *else* may we need to be able to deal with?' When the 'unexpected' comes directly from your training event participants, they already have a sense of ownership of it, and are all the more willing to try to work out ways of handling it.

7 **Be prepared for the unexpected.** As a training event facilitator, be ready for all the things which *could* happen – overhead projector bulbs blowing, power cuts, a pneumatic drill starting up outside the window, coffee not arriving at all, and so on. Always have something else in mind which can limit the damage of the unexpected.

8 **Capitalize on the unexpected.** Shamelessly draw learning points from ways that the unexpected has been successfully handled. Participants will remember the way that you, for example, turned the three fire-alarms (due to a fault in the circuit) in one morning into a learning exercise! One of us recently insisted that the fire-bells needed to be at least 20 decibels more audible in a training room to meet occupational health and safety standards!

9 **Remember that the unexpected is *shared*.** The unexpected can help bring you closer to your participants. It can help you confirm your role as 'benevolent leader'. It can help them gain respect for your judgement and decisiveness.

10 **Always have 'Plan B'!** When it is quite clear that unexpected factors have made your original plan unworkable, let it show that all the time you had in mind an alternative way for the aims of your training session to be achieved.

28

Develop participants' creativity

So often throughout our education system we have been asked for *one* right answer or correct solution. This leads to linear thinking. Being more creative is a valuable skill, and can generate new ideas as well as being fun. The Nobel-prize winning physician Albert Szent-Gyorgyi put it well: 'Discovering consists of looking at the same thing as everyone else and thinking something different.'

1 **Research participants' creativity.** Ask participants when was the last time they came up with a creative idea. What was it? What motivates them to be creative?

2 **Get spoiled for choice.** The best way to get a good idea is to have lots of ideas to choose from. For example, put a paperclip on the overhead projector, and ask participants to think of how many innovative ways they could use a paperclip. Highly successful companies encourage creativity, even though most ideas may be non-runners.

3 **Give participants a creativity-centred problem.** For example, ask them how a sheet of newspaper could be placed on the floor so that people standing face-to-face on the paper could not touch each other. No string allowed! (Solution in footnote[1].)

4 **Give participants a situation to improve.** For example, show them a picture of a tin bath with a duck floating on the water it contains. Ask them to think of as many ways of improving the situation to create an ideal bathroom as they can.

[1] Put the newspaper beneath a closed door!

5   **Mind your language!** When you respond to participants' creative ideas, be aware of the limiting effect that the following phrases could have: 'Good answer', 'That's the correct solution', 'Be practical!', 'Follow the rules', 'That's not logical'. Use open language, not 'final' language where possible; for example, 'Good, how else could this be done?'

6   **Ask 'what if?' questions.** A few questions for starters include:

- what if all 21-year-olds grew to 7 feet over the next 12 months?
- what if all men had babies?
- what if we had no seasons and it snowed all year?
- what if all women over 21 had size 8 feet?
- what if absolutely everyone did not smoke at all?
- what if everyone ate a bowl of All Bran for breakfast every day?

7   **Get participants' blood flowing!** For example, when participants have been sitting for a while, put up an alphabet in large letters on an overhead or flipchart, with 'l' and 'r' under each at random, like this:

A	B	C	D	E	G
l	r	r	r	l	l

Then get everyone to read out the alphabet together, but raising left legs if there's an 'l' and right legs if there's an 'r'!

8   **Think in metaphors.** Turn the current problem into a metaphor; for example, 'How is motivating your team like climbing a mountain?'

9   **Think how great people may have done it.** Ask your participants for the names of great people, leaders, thinkers. Ask them then how *they* might have solved particular problems, and how they might have publicized their successes.

10 **Widen horizons.** For example, ask participants what it would be like if the following pairs went for lunch together, and what they would learn from each other: 'bus driver and solicitor', 'librarian and lawyer', 'teacher and astronaut', 'air-traffic controller and politician', 'manager and newspaper editor', and so on.

29

Working one-to-one

Training events are usually group sessions. However, the things that many participants remember best are those moments when they received your individual attention. The following suggestions may help you to bring individuality to group sessions.

1 **Remember that each participant is an individual.** Everyone has their own expectations, views and aims. Try to make time to research these and to respond to them.

2 **Don't let plenary discussions degenerate into one-to-one debates!** Use coffee-breaks and meal breaks to handle issues where you really need to (or want to) enter into relatively private discussions with individual participants.

3 **Extract the issues and matters arising.** Turn individuals' questions and views into things that the whole group can become involved in.

4 **Don't take sides in public – avoid making enemies!** Acknowledge issues, questions and problems publicly, and plan to address them with the whole group as your training event proceeds.

5 **Choose your times to speak to participants privately.** When your participants are engaged in individual work or small-group work, it is often better to approach particular participants whom you know need specific advice or guidance, rather than doing so in the middle of plenary sessions.

6 **Bring everyone in.** When there is an issue or debate where one or two participants have strong views, avoid dialogues. Clarify the contending points of view, and allow the whole group to indicate the prevailing feeling on the issues.

7 **Offer to talk to individuals later.** When a problem is identified by a single participant, it can sometimes be better to offer to resolve it outside your training event, than to bring it into the limelight.

8 **Spare individual participants' feelings.** When you need to disagree with their views, it is better to do so privately than in public. Breaks in training events are sometimes the most important times – and are particularly useful for resolving difficulties or problems.

9 **Get close to anyone you really need to talk to.** Don't try to address an individual participant with a problem 'from the front'. Walk right up to them and talk to them quite quietly. If you're standing and they're sitting, you're already at an advantage!

10 **Remind everyone that you're just one person – not the management!** Help each individual participant see that your own views are those of an individual, and not automatically 'right' or 'authoritative'.

30

Help people learn from feedback

We learn a great deal from the comments we get from other people about things we do and things we try. Bring this natural way of learning into your training events.

1 **Remind participants how much we all learn from other people's comments.** Ask them to think of something about themselves they feel good about, then to jot down a few words about how they *know* they feel good about this. Their answers will often involve 'other people's comments or reactions' – in other words, feedback.

2 **Help people accept positive feedback.** Encourage participants to accept compliments. Advise them that it is unproductive to modestly 'shrug off praise'; it is better to accept it and swell with pride! This way, people are encouraged to continue to give positive feedback, rather than being embarrassed at having their comments rejected.

3 **Help participants accept negative feedback too.** Advise that there is no such thing as criticism – it should all be regarded as feedback! Explain the benefits of listening until as much as possible has been learned from constructive feedback, rather than going on the defensive and stemming the feedback, missing what could have been learned.

4 **Provide participants with opportunities to give each other feedback.** Getting people to work in pairs or in groups helps to allow participants to discuss each other's ideas, and helps to develop confidence in giving feedback.

5 **Give 'expert witness' feedback when appropriate.** Participants will wish to have your views on important issues, as you are the facilitator of the training event. But be careful that they don't regard you as an authority on everything!

6 **Gather feedback yourself from participants.** Lead by example – show participants how you can be receptive to their feedback, and accept it, whether positive or negative.

7 **Persuade participants to actively seek feedback.** Help them to become better at asking leading questions so that other people will give them reactions and comments about their performance or achievements.

8 **Help participants to use non-verbal feedback.** Alert them to the value of facial expressions and body-language as means of gathering feedback. Also, don't forget to use these sources of feedback yourself as you facilitate their learning.

9 **Build feedback sessions into your training events.** These can be sessions where participants not only tell you how they think the sessions are going but, more importantly, tell you how they are feeling about the training event, the topics and themselves.

10 **Make it all right to have 'feelings'.** Often we have feelings about things which we have not yet rationalized, but the feelings are every bit as real as our logical thoughts. Encourage participants to share their feelings and to make their feelings known. 'How do you feel about this?' is a very useful discussion-starter!

31

Help participants make sense of what they're learning

An essential component in successful learning is to 'make sense of' what has been learned – in other words, to *digest* it. Here are some suggestions to help your training event participants get to grips with the content of your programmes.

1 **Remind participants of the need to make their learning their own.** If they merely regard what they are learning as someone else's ideas, they are unlikely to ever really believe in what they learn.

2 **Give participants time.** 'Digesting' some new ideas is not done instantly. People need time to get used to new ideas or new concepts. Plan training event activities which give participants that vital time to get used to new things.

3 **Help participants to learn by explaining.** There's often no quicker way to get a grip on something new than to try and explain it to someone else. The act of explaining something necessarily involves getting one's own mind around it.

4 **Ask participants to put it in their own words.** This helps them get a sense of ownership of things they are learning – and they will usually remember their own words rather more successfully than our words!

5 **Give participants the chance to apply what they've just learned.** There's nothing better than trying out a new skill or idea to begin to understand what it really means.

6   **Get participants to make summaries.** It's all too easy for us to try to do the summing up, but it's very useful to engage participants in such processes. Let *them* decide what they think the main learning points are, or the principal ideas to remember. Asking participants to make a mind-map of what they've learned is a useful ploy.

7   **Prepare your own reviews as handouts.** It's useful if you can give your training event participants a digest of the main things from the training event as seen by you. But don't issue such handouts till the end – or better still by mail after the training event! Don't undervalue participants' own personal reviews.

8   **Help participants identify 'what this means to me'.** The real understanding comes when we relate what we have learned to the situations we encounter in our own everyday lives or jobs.

9   **Remind participants that understanding can come later than competence.** We can often learn to do things effectively, quite some time before we really understand why we are being effective. There is no shame in allowing understanding to happen in the time that it takes to happen.

10 **Aim for 'the peace that passeth understanding!'** Sooner or later, when we have really understood something, we feel 'easy' with it – and then we are all the better as trainers to begin to extend our understanding to others.

32

Presentations – if you must!

How much have *you* learned by being talked at? How many of the people whose presentations or lectures *you* attended were riveting, life-changing and real learning experiences? The usual answer is 'few'! Here are some ways of making sure that you don't do to your trainees what has often been done to you.

1 **Have a very clear purpose for any presentation you give.** Make the aims clear at the start, and sum them up again at the finish.

2 **Remember how short concentration spans are.** Members of your audience can concentrate for a few minutes now and then – but no one can concentrate for as long as you (or the authors!) sometimes like to speak. Build in 'brain breaks' at least hourly!

3 **Put it in print.** Giving your audience handout copies of the main ideas you wish to share with them can help you avoid going into too much detail. In fact, it is often better to give them the print, then turn the presentation-slot into a 'question-and-answer' session, rather than just to amplify the facts as a presentation.

4 **Sometimes participants want to sit and listen?** Yes indeed, but often as a work-avoidance strategy! After all, it is easier, if more boring, to sit and listen to a presentation than to do some real learning.

5 **Remember that it's up to them.** You may see your role as delivering a training event – but the real measure of success is how much your participants learn during it. Just doing 'your bit' doesn't necessarily mean they do 'their bit'.

6 **Watch yourself presenting.** There are few things more sobering or salutary than seeing ourselves on video giving a presentation! Make sure that at least once a year you arrange to see yourself as others see you. This can reduce the urge to give presentations quite significantly!

7 **Value the experience around you.** Often, the combined experience of participants at your training events will be very great. Don't tell people things they already know – give them the chance to tell each other what they know.

8 **Make presentations active learning experiences.** There are all sorts of ways of involving your audience in what you're presenting. The most useful tool is a good list of questions for which you can draw answers from your audience. This gives them the ownership of success.

9 **Capture your best presentations.** When you know you've got a short presentation off to a fine art, make a video of it. You can then use the video as a training event tool, and additionally be there as 'expert witness' to address questions arising from the content of the video. This can also give you a chance to recover your voice during an extended training event!

10 **Get other people to do short presentations, instead of you!** If you're working over several days with participants, a change of presenter will be a relief to them (no disrespect!). Also, you can ensure that other people introduce elements to your training event that you intend to address.

33

Using syndicates and activities

In most training events, for at least part of the time you'll want participants to work together in small groups on particular tasks. When setting up participant activities, the better you plan the briefings, the better will be the outcomes. The following suggestions may help you get the most from activities, syndicates and role plays.

1 **Make the task briefings short and clear.** Don't just give them orally – you will be surprised how many different interpretations participants can give to spoken instructions! Issue the task as a handout, or show it on the OHP or flipchart.

2 **Set a definite report-back time.** '11.27' works better than 'in half an hour please'! It usually pays to visit each syndicate in turn telling them when, say, 15, 10 and 5 minutes are left.

3 **When appropriate, form syndicates quickly and decisively!** For example, if you have your participants' names written on an overhead transparency, you can write 'A', 'B', 'C' and so on beside each name. This is quicker than saying, 'Now please would you go into groups of about five'. However, when using some activities such as role plays, you may wish to let syndicates self-select their membership.

4 **Consider rotating syndicate membership for successive activities.** This helps avoid any one syndicate suffering all the time from the least helpful participant, and spreads the skills of the most-experienced participants. Using the same overhead, you can simply write a different combination of letters beside the names for Task 2 than you used for Task 1, and so on.

5 **Sometimes, give different syndicates different activities.** This can help report-back sessions be more interesting and less repetitive. You can put participants into groups, then either give out the tasks, or let the syndicates bid for which task they are most interested in from your menu.

6 **Visit syndicates, stopping work-avoidance behaviour!** Many groups of people, left to their own devices, can chat *about* the work they're supposed to be doing for many minutes without ever starting to do it. Suggest that they brainstorm ideas for the first five minutes, writing everything on a flipchart.

7 **Anticipate how you want the report-back stage to go.** Specify to syndicates what you will ask them to do when their task is completed; for example, to talk through an overhead they've prepared, or a flipchart. Discourage purely verbal outcomes – these are transient and valuable things may be lost.

8 **Experiment with syndicate-owned tasks.** Once you've got syndicates working well, you can give groups five minutes to write on an overhead the task they want to set themselves for the next 30 minutes. Then briefly let the whole group see the range of tasks so everyone knows what everyone else is doing.

9 **Chair report-back sessions brutally!** There are always some participants who will wish to read out to the whole group words that can already be seen on overheads or flipcharts. Giving syndicates, say, two minutes only can help avoid this, and help them to focus on key outcomes or issues. Ask for a volunteer timekeeper.

10 **Avoid chipping in with too many answers.** Let each group report back before you bridge any gaps. Give participants the chance to gain full ownership of the ideas that emerge from their syndicate work.

34

Using 'home groups'

Particularly at extended training events lasting several days, participants may be spending considerable time in groups doing tasks. In such cases, it's useful to have a 'home group' which meets periodically throughout the event.

1 **Explain the rationale for having 'home groups'.** Explain to participants that their home groups will remain the same in composition throughout the course, and that in these groups they can share ideas or problems they find with their work in other groups addressing specific tasks during the course.

2 **Promote 'ownership' of home groups.** It is often best if these groups do not have a named facilitator or rapporteur. It is usually enough to give the home groups clear briefings regarding the outcomes they are intended to produce at each stage in your course.

3 **Whenever possible, let home groups constitute themselves.** It can be useful if you can find one way or another of allowing participants to choose which home group they will belong to. This can, for example, be on the basis of experience, or simply shared interests.

4 **Give home groups clear tasks to do.** As your course progresses, ensure that whatever else home groups do, they address particular tasks at each meeting. Make it clear that they can also address any other tasks they think of – but not at the expense of missing out the 'named' task for the meeting.

5 **Give home groups opportunities to report back.** It often helps to make such groups productive if they know that they will have five minutes at a forthcoming plenary to share the products of their thinking and work.

6 **Encourage home groups to develop their own product.** For example, set home groups an ongoing task at the start of your course, and invite them to build up data and evidence to support their findings on the task, and to share all of this towards the end of the course.

7 **Allow home groups to be different.** It can be much more productive when home groups are working on different tasks or ideas, rather than all doing the same thing in parallel.

8 **Give home groups sufficient time.** It is not enough to have short meetings in between the principal parts of your course. Giving a group a relatively short task to complete in a whole hour can mean that the group goes on to do a lot of useful thinking around and beyond the immediate content of the training event.

9 **Give one important thing (at least) entirely to home groups.** This shows that you value their work. Make sure that the products of their work on this task will be part of any overall collection of the outcomes of your course.

10 **Make sure that home groups have a home.** Try to ensure that they will always meet in the same place, to start with, at least, and if possible try to generate a more 'homely' atmosphere for these meetings, for example by arranging that do-it-yourself facilities are available for the making of tea and coffee.

35

Using role plays

The benefits of using role-play exercises can be considerable. However, there are risks too, and some trainers are rather afraid of using them. Participants may also have mixed feelings about the prospect of becoming intimately involved in some role-play situations. We hope the following suggestions will help you strike the right balance.

1   **Consider the benefits of using role plays.** You can choose to get participants enacting some of the most difficult aspects of the topic they're addressing – yet in the privacy of a small group and in a supportive environment.

2   **Remember the dangers of role playing.** It's possible for participants sometimes to get 'too involved' in the role play, and personal feelings can become inflamed or hurt. Therefore, it is often wise to be careful in selecting which participants may be asked to take on certain roles.

3   **Explain a bit about role playing.** If everyone knows that they are not playing themselves, but are deliberately adopting a 'stance' in a role play, they are more likely to be able to do so effectively and without their feelings getting in the way.

4   **Keep an eye on activities and role plays.** Be ready to enter in or even intervene, if you think that something is in danger of getting out of hand, or is going off at a tangent to the intended purpose.

5   **Capitalize on printed 'briefings' for roles.** Keep these short, however. For example, in a role play involving, say, four players, have an A5 card, with the key information on it for each of the participants.

6   **Decide whether briefings will be shared or private.** Sometimes a role play works best when everyone fully knows the roles that other people are playing. At other times, the element of surprise may be needed, and it can be useful for aspects of the respective roles to be kept hidden until the right moment.

7 **Consider 'fishbowling' a role play.** In such cases, you can choose participants (or let them self-select) on the basis of people who are comfortable to give the role play a try.

8 **Think about the possibility of using closed circuit television, if available.** When you want to have a chosen group run through a role play exercise, but without everyone watching them directly, you may be able to have the role play itself occurring in an 'intimate' environment, while being viewed by the rest of the group using CCTV, enabling the group to discuss the role play as it occurs.

9 **Debrief role play activities carefully.** Help participants to separate the feelings they had during the role play from the learning outcomes that the role play led to.

10 **Always come back to the objectives of a role play.** Sometimes, you may have decided not to reveal these in detail until the end anyway. It helps a lot if participants can see that there were definite and valuable purposes in getting them involved in a role play – especially if there were some tense moments during its execution!

36

End with a bang!

There's nothing worse than when a training event just seems to fizzle out! Or when participants seem to slip out one-by-one, and only the keen ones remain till the end. Of such things are nightmares made. Here are some ways to bring your training events to successful conclusions.

1 **Keep your eye on the time, so you can end promptly.** This means also not trying to cram in to the last hour all the things you wished you'd said during the whole training event.

2 **Avoid long 'general discussion' or 'matters arising' sessions.** It's tempting to round off training programmes with such sessions, but it's best to deliberately keep them quite short.

3 **Get everyone to contribute in final plenaries.** Avoid the normal happening of two or three participants having a lot to say, and other people getting fed up of hearing them! Use rounds of short, sharp questions, asking everyone for their answers or show-of-hands votes.

4 **Save something for participants to do near the end.** For example, give them each an action planning sheet, a few minutes to make individual plans, then a few minutes to compare their plans with each other.

5 **Have something important to give participants at the end.** Save one of your handouts to pass round then – especially one which sums up most of the things that have been covered by your training event.

6 **Encourage participants to stay in touch.** Where your participants come from different places or sites, it can be useful to get them all to put their phone numbers onto a single sheet, then circulate this sheet to them afterwards along with any other papers arising from the products of their activities during your training event.

7 **Gather your own feedback.** Find out what participants' first impressions of the training event are. You can always gather the more considered impressions later too. Remember, however, that their immediate impressions can change when they come to try to implement the things that your training event was intended to help them become able to do.

8 **Remind participants what they've done.** Go back to the aims of the training event and the expectations of the participants, and help them to see what has been achieved. If necessary, flipchart a list of 'matters outstanding' which could maybe be addressed by a further event.

9 **Remember to thank your participants.** Thank them for their work during the training event, and their cooperation at achieving the aims of the programme.

10 **Have a further round of tea/coffee/juice at the end.** This can allow participants who need to get away promptly to leave when the training event finishes, and can also allow those who would like to talk further to you or to each other to do so for as long as they wish.

Chapter 5 Looking After Yourself

In this chapter, we've collected suggestions which are mainly designed to help *you*! Of course, all of this book is meant to help you one way or another, but here we particularly wanted to offer ideas for keeping your sanity and dignity. Most things in this chapter we learned by getting it wrong at some stage. We are particularly pleased to include in this chapter about 30 suggestions contributed by our friend and colleague Sally Brown (who has run training events across the planet, and is therefore particularly appropriate for giving tips for international trainers).

'Be ever-ready!' includes details of the sorts of things that you wished you'd packed when you got your bits and pieces ready for an event!

'Getting yourself organized' is specifically about *your* comfort. When you're feeling relaxed and well, you run training events rather better than when you're feeling stressed and tense.

'Keeping up to date' is another aspect of looking after yourself, this time in the context of making sure that your career and job prospects are well attended to.

'Dealing with difficult questions' is of course a topic that could have gone into Chapter 4, but we thought it best to put it in the present chapter, as being well-able to handle difficult questions is really important for we trainers – as well as for our participants. Similarly, when dealing with difficult participants, probably the most important thing is that we emerge unscathed and unrattled.

You may be surprised to find some suggestions on 'body language' in this chapter, but we think you'll agree that our suggestions have your best interests at heart!

'Filling five minutes to coffee!' is often a task where the main purpose is to look after ourselves rather than our participants! If participants have

nothing to do and have to wait around until the coffee arrives, it under-
mines what we have been doing with them before the break.

Finally, the 'Tips for international trainers' speak for themselves. Don't
worry, however, if you don't think you're going to take your training programmes to remote corners of the globe – many of these tips also apply to
going on holiday!

37

Be ever-ready!

Carry your case of bits and bobs with you at all times. Being prepared is the motto of the effective trainer. How many times have you asked for materials to be available, only to find they were not provided?

1 **Get a box!** Invest in a creative box or carry-case or container that you can take anywhere.

2 **Get the size right!** If you're travelling mostly by car, you can afford to take with you a bigger box than you may be able to carry on trains or on foot or in the air.

3 **Be secure!** Think about the best way to keep your bits and pieces from getting mixed up in transit. Make sure that separate things can be kept in separate parts of your kit. Have you noticed how inconvenient it is when Blu-tack, pens and pencils become intimate in your kit?

4 **Label everything.** Make sure that all your bits and pieces have your name, work address, phone/fax number on them. This way, you're likely to get back the things you leave behind in the hurry of departure!

5 **Have everything with you!** This can profitably include Blu-tack, OHP pens, flipchart pens, scissors, spare paper, paper clips, drawing pins, tissues (you may make some participants cry!), string, sticky labels, a clock, pins, sunglasses (for when the group adjourns to the lawn on a hot day), safety pins (you never know when you, or a participant, will really need one!), a toothbrush, an eraser, peppermints, headache tablets, chalk, blank transparencies, Sellotape, even a set of jump leads and a complete British Rail timetable. Don't forget either how useful a couple of screwdrivers can turn out to be, including a Phillips one.

6 **Make a checklist.** For each event, make a list of the things you know you may need, and tick them off as you check you've got them in your box. You can also use this list to check that you've collected back everything at the end of your session.

7 **Avoid rummaging!** When searching for a particular item from your kit, choose a moment when participants are busy, rather than watching you search!

8 **Add to your inventory.** There will always be *something* that you wished you'd brought with you. Next time, you can.

9 **Actions speak louder than words!** Always have one or two exercises that you can give participants to do when you need to gather your own thoughts. Have handouts or briefings for such activities included in your kit.

10 **Never leave home without one!** As you build up your experience, keep a bag packed with all the things that *you*, not your participants, find you may need on an away-trip of a couple of days or a week. Look after yourself, and you'll look after your participants all the better!

38

Getting yourself organized

It's worth spending a bit of time planning how you will look after yourself, both on the way to your session and while running it. Trainers often have to travel for their work, and getting the arrangements right can make all the difference to your training events. The following tips are gleaned from the hard school of experience (often getting things wrong!)

1 **Research your travel arrangements carefully.** Fix start and finish times of training events to fit in with your travel plans. Being able to catch the 05.05 train may make your life much easier than travelling just ten minutes later. Book your taxi at lunchtime for the homeward journey.

2 **Avoid travelling to the venue on the actual day whenever possible.** Travelling the night before can reduce undue stress on the day itself.

3 **Travel light.** Stick to a good smart suit or jacket and ring the changes with a variety of blouses/shirts when you are away for several days.

4 **Wear really comfortable shoes.** You may be on your feet for long periods of the day and it does not help if they are aching.

5 **Specify really clearly to your client what you expect to be available in the training room.** Don't expect everything to be there without question. Put your requirements in writing – don't just rely on telephoned reassurances!

6 **Allow enough time at the beginning of the session to check equipment and materials.** Give yourself the comfort that you will have time to ask for further supplies if necessary. Have a checklist ready, including such things as overhead projector, blank transparencies, OHP pens, video playback equipment, audiotape machine, slide projector, flipchart and plenty of flipchart paper, flipchart pens, markerboard pens and wiper, drawing paper, Blu-tack, masking tape, Sellotape, chalk, scissors, index cards, and so on. (In another set of tips – 37 – we've suggested items for your own basic portable kit too.)

7 **Specify in writing (or check) the times for lunch, tea and coffee.** Double-check these times on arrival – nothing messes up your timings as much as late refreshment breaks. If your client doesn't supply lunch for you, research your own arrangements or take your own lunch.

8 **Keep a supply of mints and/or throat pastilles with you.** This can save you the embarrassment of voice problems during your training event. Ensuring you have a drink of water available also helps. Other useful emergency aids include aspirin, tissues, spare tights (if appropriate), a spare tie (if appropriate), and a dram for the journey home (often very appropriate!)

9 **Pace yourself.** When your participants are 'on task', sit down and wait for them to ask for help. Don't walk about and interrupt their tasks too much. Save your energy for the parts where you need to be dynamic.

10 **Keep your stress levels down.** Don't let yourself get flustered by people who arrive late, disappear for parts of your session, leave early, or who are obviously upset or worried by things outside your training event or your control. Stay calm and concentrate on the training session.

(The authors are particularly grateful to Sally Brown for contributing this set of tips, and faxing them from New Zealand – see also her contributions on international trips!)

39

Keeping up to date

It is all too easy to get caught up in the design and delivery of training events at the expense of building in time for our own professional development.

1   **Subscribe to a journal.** Try and subscribe to at least one journal which will help you to keep up to date with developments. If you can, form local or regional groups, so that each group member can subscribe to a different journal, then circulate it round group members.

2   **Search the Internet.** This is exciting technology for those who have access to it. At one coffee shop in London you can search the World Wide Web – good value for a cup of coffee! As more people become involved with such technology, more information becomes freely available. If you're not familiar with how to use the World Wide Web, book yourself onto a training session!

3   **Trainers do it with books!** Try to read a new book at least every two months. Look out for book reviews in appropriate journals to help guide your reading. While travelling between jobs, spend half an hour in the nearest bookshop. Don't forget to use your local library too, and any college or university whose library you have easy access to.

4   **Start a reflective journal.** One way of keeping up to date is by reflecting on what we do currently. Fairly promptly after each session you run, write down things that went particularly well, and things that were not so successful. Jot down questions to yourself about your practice. Also, reflect back, and jot down changes you have made on the basis of experience.

5   **View a new video every couple of months.** Build time in your diary to make use of such resources. Find out how to get to see material on video, for example in libraries, or learning resources centres in colleges or companies. Swap your own videos with visiting colleagues.

6 **Join a trainers' e-mail network.** Many new networks are starting up on the Internet. If there isn't yet one in your own specialist area, think of starting one yourself. If you haven't got Internet facilities, ask your boss when you may expect your organization to get itself connected! With a computer, a modem and some software, you could set yourself up from home.

7 **Talk to colleagues.** It is amazing how much useful information we can all pick up simply by talking to friends and colleagues. Ask them about their latest 'best read', the most interesting recent article they've seen, the best session they've done recently.

8 **Travel with a talking book.** These cover a whole host of topics and are available freely from local libraries. They can be a wonderful asset on boring journeys to work, or when stuck in the inevitable traffic jams. You can even listen to them when undertaking your stress management programme on the exercise bike or the cross-country ski machine!

9 **Rank the 'Trainers top ten conferences'.** Conferences seem to be advertised around every corner and in every envelope that comes into the in-tray. Ask around, and get to know the conferences that consistently offer good programmes. Use conferences to find people to network with. You don't have to attend conferences to derive at least some benefit from them; for example, follow up reviews of conferences and obtain the proceedings of useful ones if they are published.

10 **Gain an additional qualification.** We're never too old to learn! There are so many exciting courses around. Even those that don't lead to a qualification can do wonders to recharge our batteries, and to help us discover new like-minded people.

40

Dealing with difficult questions

A 'difficult' question tends to be one where we don't know the answer, or where there are several ways of approaching the question and we don't know which way is best! Our training events are often judged on the basis of the way we demonstrate our professionalism when faced with such questions.

1 **Don't try to pretend you have an answer when you haven't!** We've all dug ourselves into deep holes in such situations. It is far better to admit, 'I'm not at all sure I can answer this one right now' than to waffle and fudge.

2 **Clarify the question.** Help your participants work out exactly what the question means, breaking it down if necessary into separate parts needing separate answers. Write up the agreed version of the question on a flipchart, so everyone can see the words and reflect on the agreed version of the question.

3 **Ask for volunteers from your participants.** Often, when there's a difficult question, there will be one or more participants who have more idea than we have about how the question could be approached.

4 **Give participants some privacy to explore a difficult question.** When such a question is really important, it is worth spending some time where participants in groups can informally brainstorm ways of approaching the question. The report-backs from the groups can retain a degree of anonymity about particular ideas which emerge during the group discussions.

5 **Turn difficult questions into an ongoing agenda.** Especially at residential training events, it is often worth writing up difficult questions on flipcharts and leaving them on the wall, asking anyone with ideas about how to tackle the questions to write their ideas on post-its, and stick them onto the respective flipcharts. They can choose to do this anonymously, by sticking the post-its up during breaks or overnight!

6 **Expect that there will be no 'right answer' to a difficult question.** Such questions tend to have a range of alternative answers. Affirm that its OK *not* to have a ready answer to such a question. Try to collect as many alternative solutions to a problem as possible.

7 **Get participants to 'rate' alternative answers.** For each alternative approach ask, 'What's the best thing going about this approach?' and, 'What's the biggest danger with this approach?'

8 **Offer to find out some answers to difficult questions within a week or two.** For example, offer to consult colleagues in the field concerned. Summarize their responses to the questions, and circulate the summary to your participants.

9 **Welcome difficult questions!** Don't try to divert participants back to the things you intended them to do next. Say words to the effect, 'I'm so glad this came up. It's really important and worth exploring now. Thank you for raising the issue.'

10 **Build on your experience.** Next time you run a similar training event, build in the difficult questions as case studies or examples, armed with the thinking that you and previous participants have already done. A training event which tackles difficult questions head-on will be seen as much more useful to participants than one which tries to skirt round problematic areas.

41

Dealing with difficult participants

However enthusiastic you are about your subject, you will sometimes find yourself faced with handling difficult people and difficult reactions. There is usually at least one such person – usually in the back right-hand corner! Interpret such reactions with care. We all have difficult days – whether we overslept, or tripped over the cat, or got a further electric bill reminder!

1 **Don't have a back right-hand corner in the first place!** When participants are sitting in a circle or a U-shape, it's less likely that someone who may become difficult establishes the right sort of territory to become difficult!

2 **Stop, and bring the difficult participant into play.** Say words along the lines of, 'I think our colleague here has concerns about what we're doing. Would you like to share them with us all?' Sometimes, people are only difficult when they feel their views are not being considered.

3 **Remember aggressive behaviour may indicate insecurities.** When some people are insecure they curl up and go into their shells, but others react in a much more 'open' and aggressive way. Try carefully to find out what might be the cause of their behaviour. They could be apprehensive about a new item or idea you are trying to introduce, or a new way of working. If possible, use a coffee break to try to probe the real cause of any problem.

4 **Be firm if necessary.** If you really find you've got a round peg in a square hole, you may consider politely suggesting (during a break, not publicly) that if the training event and its pre-declared objectives don't meet the participant's requirements, it may be best to leave, and offer to refund any fee.

5 **Try to involve everyone.** Some people may be difficult because they feel left out or marginalized. Frequent small-group activities can dispel anxieties and get most people involved. Busy people have less time to worry.

6 **Quieten the overzealous question-asker.** One person who tries to dominate the conversation and asks incessant questions can cause annoyance to others who feel their time is being wasted or that the discussion is going off at a tangent. Watch your audience carefully to pick up the group or individual reactions. When necessary, say something along the lines of, 'Thank you very much for all these interesting questions, however, we must press on now if we are to finish on time.'

7 **Tackle the problem head-on.** Say something like, 'Would you like to share your problem with the group?' If you feel that openness would not work, ask *everyone* to jot down one concern or worry they may have. Collect in the questions and issues, and deal with them without naming the originators. Many group members may be pleased that issues have been brought out into the open in this way.

8 **Don't disagree with a person – only ideas or views.** 'I don't think this would work in practice' is a diplomatic alternative to, 'I think that's a silly idea!' Try to avoid showing favouritism. It is human nature to gravitate towards some people more than others. However, anyone who senses that you don't like them is likely to engage in open hostility. Work hard at treating everyone equally.

9 **Turn the difficulty into fun.** People don't like their serious objections turned into a joke! However, only do this if you really have tried as many constructive tactics as you can think of. Humbling a difficult participant in this way creates a real enemy for the rest of the training event!

10 **Take a 'brain-break'.** When tempers are getting frayed or discussions becoming heated, little will be achieved. That can be a good time to suggest a walkabout, or comfort break, or a chance to view materials. It provides cooling off time too.

42

Body language

Whether you are talking to 200 people in a large lecture room or training a small group of people, it is important to consider your use of body language. Watching your participants carefully can give you some very useful indications of how they are feeling, and your own body language can help you show your group how you are feeling.

1 **Maintain eye-contact with your group.** This helps to establish a positive relationship with participants. Looking people in the eye along with a smile can help to relax folk as they enter your room. Remember, some may be feeling apprehensive, not knowing quite what to expect.

2 **Avoid looking over people's heads.** They will start to turn round to see what is on the back wall! Equally, don't spend too much time watching the floor; some participants may begin to feel left out – or think that the carpet is magic!

3 **Avoid looking at the same person all the time** (even when a friendly face). It is tempting to focus our attention on the person directly in front of us. It is easy to miss out people sitting on your far left or far right, and occasionally you may need to position your body directly towards these groups to avoid them feeling left out.

4 **Watch your hands!** Swinging them around your body with great enthusiasm can be distracting to some. Holding them firmly clasped behind your back can indicate a 'royal stance'! If you are feeling nervous, you may find yourself clasping your hands in front of you as though they are about to drop off. Remember that those in the front row see the close-up view. Also, if your hands shake when you're nervous, try not to write directly onto the OHP, where shakes are magnified ten-fold!

5 **Avoid hiding your hands in pockets** (especially when the pockets contain coins or keys). It is amazing the sounds we can create – but which we don't hear ourselves – when we are busy thinking of the next things we are going to say. By the time we have finished saying it, someone will have worked out exactly how much money is in our pocket!

6 **Think about what you are wearing.** You may think that your patched jeans and 'holey' T-shirt are the latest fashion – but others may perceive you differently. Think carefully about the culture of the organization where you're working. In some, casual wear is the norm, but in others it may be perceived as not paying respect to tradition.

7 **Video yourself, and reflect on your body language.** Do you move around too much, or stand glued to the floor? It is sobering (and often painful) to see ourselves as others see us. It is always useful. It is valuable to gather feedback from your group too.

8 **Avoid standing too close to any one person.** Remember there are social distance zones. If we encroach too far into these zones, people will back-off or misinterpret our intentions. Also, be aware of different cultural norms. What is considered a normal body-distance zone in one culture can be a threatening one in another.

9 **Watch the position of your body.** Turning sideways when talking to someone may give the message that you're not really interested in the conversation. Folding your arms may be perceived as being defensive. Walking up and down the room too much could indicate you're nervous (or have an attack of pins and needles!)

10 **Interpret the body language of others with caution!** Fiddling with cuffs or collars may not necessarily indicate nervousness – it could be a case of a button that is about to fall off! Crossed arms can be a comfortable position for many: only take care when they are accompanied by crossed legs and a frown!

43

Filling five minutes to coffee!

It is always useful to have a collection of 'fillers' up your sleeve. However well we try to plan our time, situations will occur when it is really not worth starting on that new or different topic area. Try not to prolong an activity or topic just for the sake of it.

1 **'Design a poster in three minutes, indicating what your group has gained from the session.'** This is a good way of still maintaining the topic, and getting groups to collect their thoughts together. It can also be a lot of fun, especially if they are to produce large and colourful posters. The two final minutes can be spent viewing the products of other groups.

2 **'What have been your most positive learning experiences from the session, and why?'** Allow three minutes to write a few comments on a post-it or scrap of paper.

3 **Buy a puzzle book.** These can give you lots of ideas for little time-fillers. For example: 'A beetle goes through five volumes of an encyclopaedia, A–E, which are sitting side-by-side on a shelf. The beetle starts on page 1 of Book A, and continues to the last page of Book E. The pages of each book total 2.5 inches and each cover is 0.1 of an inch thick. How far does the beetle travel?' Mathematicians in the group are always worst at this sort of activity – so be forewarned!

4 **Ask participants for the 20 best tips for coping with stress.** We all face varying amounts of stress; some we handle better than others. What is our best method? Is it digging up all those weeds, or treating ourselves to a bag of sweets, or ten minutes on the exercise bike, or a fight with a pillow? If participants don't wish to disclose them in public, get them to write their tips down on post-its and stick them to a wall, so everyone can pick up some tips over lunch.

5   **Reward your participants for working hard.** We are all so busy leading our own lives, and meeting all those work deadlines, that we sometimes forget to say 'thank you' to those who help us. Brainstorm as many ways as possible of saying 'Thank you'. Then vote on the three most useful suggestions. It is amazing how creative your participants may be with this activity, especially when they know lunch is about to be served!

6   **'What do you hope to achieve in 12 months time?'** Give everyone an envelope and a small piece of paper, and ask them this. The answers can include both professional and personal ambitions and hopes. Ask individuals to seal their envelopes, and put them in a secure place or give them to a good friend, to consult again in 12 months. Suggest they put a note in their calendars or diaries to remind them to re-open their envelopes to check how many of their plans have been achieved.

7   **'What would you do with a £50 book token?'** Ask your participants to imagine they've been given such a book token to spend on the topic of your training event. What books would they buy, and why? Use this to build your own bibliography!

8   **Castaway on a desert island.** You are allowed one novel, or CD, only. What would each of your group members take, and why? Make your own presents list!

9   **'The most interesting seminar I have ever attended is. . ., because. . .'.** This exercise is a good way of building up tips for your next seminars or training events. What makes a 'gold star' training event?

10   **'Criteria for the best boss of the year award'** What makes a good boss? Remind the group that 'uneasy rests the butt on which the boss sits!' and ask them for one characteristic they would like to see in their current boss, or the best characteristic their current line manager displays. Then vote for the best three characteristics.

44

Tips for international trainers

Trainers who travel abroad frequently need to be especially well-organized and prepared. The following suggestions, gleaned from hard experience, may be helpful to you.

1 **Always carry your main training materials in your hand luggage** – even if they are quite bulky. You just can't afford for them to go missing in a lost suitcase. This is particularly true of your collection of overhead transparencies.

2 **Send out as much as you can in advance.** Send out handouts, books, overhead transparencies, and get your client to fax you an acknowledgement of their receipt, allowing yourself time to take out replacements if they don't arrive. Couriers are often only a little more expensive than the postal system, and can get things to most places within five working days.

3 **Carry one of everything important anyway.** Even when you've sent out copies of handouts or transparencies, always have enough with you to be able to generate new copies from scratch in an emergency.

4 **Think carefully about your equipment needs.** Have contingency plans in case something you ask for is not available. Even overhead projectors are not universal, and flipchart paper is unknown in some countries (newsprint makes an acceptable alternative and is widely available).

5 **Check that any electrical equipment you take is compatible with local supplies.** This particularly applies to any projection or computer equipment you may want to take with you.

6 **Remember that hot countries often have air-conditioned training facilities.** This can make your training room quite cool, so dress accordingly. It is a strange experience to be shivery while working in a tropical country!

7 **Check out local dress codes with your client.** It is almost as embarrassing to be over-formally dressed in a relaxed context as it is to be under-dressed in a formal one. You will need to consider carefully whether your clothing might offend local beliefs or customs in some countries.

8 **Be careful with acronyms.** Those familiar in your own country may be unknown in others. For example, familiar education acronyms in the UK such as SEDA, FEFCE or UCOSDA may well mean nothing to people in other countries. Spell all acronyms out, at least in the first instance.

9 **Mind your language!** In countries where the first language is not English, frame your language appropriately, avoiding excessive use of unusual or jargon words. Even audiences in English-speaking countries may find elements of what you say incomprehensible.

10 **Don't automatically expect it to be a holiday!** An international training trip can be stressful and very tiring. Don't expect to do too much sightseeing alongside your work, unless you can build in some extra days just for this.

11 **Take plenty of business cards with you.** People often want to keep contact with you after a training event – and this can develop into further opportunities for follow-up trips.

12 **On long-haul flights, don't expect to do too much work.** If you want to minimize the effects of jet lag, you need to rest and relax on the flight. Avoid too much alcohol – this in conjunction with cabin air-conditioning can be very dehydrating. Dress comfortably and in layers to cope with changing temperatures (planes can be quite cool), and exercise regularly (in the confines of the loo if necessary).

13 **Keep your emergency medical kit in your hand luggage.** This could include aspirin, diarrhoea remedies, and so on. It is frustrating to feel ill when all your medicines are safely stowed in the plane's hold!

14 **Travel as light as possible.** You need fewer clothes than most people think, and laundry facilities exist throughout the world! Take clothes that travel well and don't mind being crushed in a suitcase.

15 **Take something to eat and drink in your hand luggage.** This can be a life-saver if you are delayed for hours, maybe at an airport with no catering facilities!

16 **Think carefully about taking your laptop computer.** Check that your insurance covers international travel, and also check whether there will be suitable power supplies for it. It may be possible for you to arrange for your client to loan you a computer for the duration of your visit.

17   **Allow plenty of time in your schedule for delays.** It is not unknown to arrive at your destination 24 hours late on long trips involving several connections. Build appropriate leeway into your travel schedule.

18   **Double-check passport and visa requirements.** Find out, for example, whether you need a work permit for what you are doing. Immigration controls can be strict and draconian.

19   **Don't carry everything you're given back with you.** If you're given lots of reports, brochures, papers and so on by your client or by your participants, post them home, along with any of your own training materials that you're sure you have finished with, rather than struggling to fit them all into your luggage. But don't post anything that you could need urgently.

20   **Remember that faxes are cheaper than phones** (and faxes don't depend on the person you're contacting being 'in'). Leave your colleagues and loved ones with details of where they can fax you and when. You may be surprised how well you can remain in touch on the other side of the world. However, the phone is always worth it for that very special person!

21   **Take two watches.** If your journey is taking you to several different time-zones, it is handy to have one watch permanently set to the time in the UK. This can help ensure that you know when to catch anyone you may need to ring back at home. And you never know when your main watch may drop off in Singapore – a backup can be very useful!

22   **Don't drink Nile water!** When in countries where the public water supply may contain things your metabolism is not geared up to, stick to cool drinks from bottles or cans. Don't forget that ice-cubes can be contaminated by things your system won't cope with happily! The whisky may be fine, but the knocks can come from the rocks!

(These tips – except 22! – have been kindly contributed by our favourite famous international traveller, Sally Brown.)

Chapter 6 Evaluating your Training Events

The main way we get better at things is by finding out more about what goes right and what goes wrong. It is all too easy to be so busy planning our next training events that we shelve the task of really finding out how our last ones went. We often go as far as collecting feedback, but never really analyse it.

We start our suggestions on evaluation with ideas for gathering and using feedback during training events as well as after them. We hope you will like our idea of a 'forgettery' – this is not to do with having short memories about things that go wrong, but rather it is about consciously deciding which memories about such things to carry forward.

Our next two sets of suggestions are about designing and using questionnaires. Feedback gathered by questionnaire is particularly useful, as it is 'solid evidence' of what people think, and we can sift through the evidence as often as we wish and for as long as we wish, and interpret it in great detail. However, it is all too easy for situations to arise where people fill in questionnaires quickly and 'lightly' without thinking much about the real meaning behind the questions. We hope our suggestions will help you get the most from questionnaires, and minimize the dangers associated with them.

In 'Following-up after a training event', we particularly have in mind the sort of training event which takes participants to an end-point, but where it could be particularly useful for them to continue to network and further develop the ideas that have been introduced in the training event.

Our next two sets of suggestions are about using other ways to gather even more feedback, including seeking feedback from the managers or supervisors of the people who attend your training events.

We end this book with 'Replanning your training event'. A sign of success can be that other clients want you to run similar training events for them. In any case, you will probably have 'mainstay' training events that you tend to run at regular intervals. Either way, it's worth spending time now and then replanning such sessions, and gathering specific feedback as you run them to help you redesign them next time.

45

Obtaining feedback – and developing your forgettery!

Just as it is useful to encourage our participants to give feedback to each other, it is vital that we gather feedback from them about us. This can be painful at times! The following suggestions may help.

1 **Install a forgettery!** It's all too easy to retain the hurt from negative feedback about our performances as trainers, but it's best to consciously decide to forget the pain, and simply to carry forward practical plans for what we will do next time – and what we will avoid doing ever again.

2 **Gather feelings in advance when possible.** It is often possible to design a short pre-event questionnaire which includes questions to help you find out in advance what participants already know; it can also be used to find out a little about their existing attitudes and feelings about the theme of the training event.

3 **Ask participants how they feel.** It is often worth doing this after a meal break, or at the beginning of a new day in an extended course. All the better if their responses are not confined to their feelings about the training event or course.

4 **Put up a 'feelings chart'.** For example, stick up a flipchart in a corner of the room, and place a pad of post-its on a table. Invite participants to stick post-its with their feelings or questions onto the chart at any time during the programme. They can choose breaks in the programme to do this, especially if they prefer their feelings to remain anonymous.

5 **Ask, 'How are you finding the programme so far?'** Take care to continue smiling (and biting your tongue) when things you hear disappoint you; don't stifle feedback even when it is unwelcome. Bin the pain in your forgettery – carry forward the things you're learning.

6   **Try 'stop, start, continue'.** Especially in the middle of your training event, give out post-its and ask participants to write these three words as headings, and to give you messages about what they would like you to stop doing, start doing, and continue to do. You can respond to the 'stop' and 'start' messages during the rest of the training event.

7   **Build on positive feedback.** For example, when participants tell you to continue things in a 'stop, start, continue' round, make sure that you build in more of the same things as and when you can.

8   **Do a written training event evaluation.** It's useful to design a *short* questionnaire with a few structured (for example, tick boxes) questions, so you can get a quick impression of your participants' reactions.

9   **Also ask two or three open-ended questions.** For example, ask participants, 'What did you most like about the way the training event was run?' and, if you dare, the corresponding 'least like' question too. Again, put any pain in your forgettery, and carry forward the useful ideas for improvement.

10   **Make your own list of feedback points to yourself.** It's well worth spending a few minutes after the close of your training events jotting down notes to yourself about what you learned, and about what you would or would not try if running the same training event again tomorrow. Don't expect to keep all these thoughts in your head – jot them down, then you can relax and forget any tensions.

46

Designing good questionnaires

Questionnaires can be a really useful source of information and feedback. However, it is essential that you are really clear about the sort of information you want from a questionnaire. Preplanning and time for analysis are essential features when using them.

1   **What are you trying to achieve?** This may seem rather simplistic but it is well worth spending some time thinking about what sort of information you want to receive. It is very easy to get carried away and ask for the world.

2   **Keep it simple.** In this way you will be much more likely to get a return. How many times have you started to complete a questionnaire only to find it difficult to understand? Simple words and short sentences are more likely to get responses – and honest ones at that.

3   **Avoid jargon or acronyms.** Even acronyms like AVA, IT and OHTs may not be understood by everyone. Don't assume that your participants know the special language of your training event topic – or training terminology.

4   **Keep it short and sweet.** Decide on the length. Generally speaking, the shorter the better. Psychologically, the longer the questionnaire, the more likely we are to put it in the bin or where it gets buried under a pile of papers. In order to keep the questionnaire to one or two sides of A4 paper, do not reduce the print size so that no one without a magnifying glass or strong spectacles can read it! Instead, reduce the number of questions.

5   **Know your audience.** Think carefully about the recipients of this questionnaire. Try to make the questions as relevant and interesting to them as possible.

6   **Use some closed questions.** A closed question is where you ask for a structured response (typically yes/no) or the ticking of an appropriate box. This sort of question is normally very easy to complete and the responses easy to analyse. Remember though that participants may make 'instant' or surface decisions – especially if there are too many closed questions.

7   **Include some open questions.** There will be occasions where you want a much longer or less structured response than you get just from closed questions. Open questions, such as those including such phrases as: 'What is your opinion of. . .?', 'How have you found. . .?', 'What would you have liked. . .?', or 'What do you see happening in the future?', can elicit some very useful information.

8   **Consider one or two 'leading questions'.** We've found it useful, for example, to ask participants to tell us: 'The thing I most liked about the way the training event was run was. . .' and, 'The thing that most annoyed me about how the training event was run was. . .'. Sometimes the responses hurt – but are useful feedback none the less.

9   **Layout – first impressions count.** If the questionnaire looks professional and well set out, you will be much more likely to obtain a good response. Consider whether any of the following would help: a cartoon, different named sections, questions in boxes, answers all to be given in a right-hand column, occasional use of **bold** and *italics*, or an unusual font.

10 **Are you colour-coded?** How many 'trees' of paper come onto our desks each month, and how will anyone distinguish your questionnaire from the rest of the pile? Think about using a different colour of paper – green, blue – or maybe better, sepia or peach. Pages of different colours seem to 'hit us in the eye' and almost demand our attention.

47

Using questionnaires well

Having spent time designing good questionnaires, it is worth devoting some thought to piloting them, and deciding how best to put them to use.

1 **Questionnaire designers do it with a friend.** Always trial your questionnaire first. It does involve extra time which needs to be built into the planning process, but it is well worth the extra effort. You may just want to check that the questions are understandable to a colleague or neighbour. If, however, your circulation is large and the questionnaire is really important, you may need to pilot it with between ten and 50 people. This will usually lead you towards making some valuable modifications.

2 **Give it out at the end, and collect immediately?** This has the benefit that you can get a complete set of feedback, but the drawback is that the feedback may be coloured by the feelings of the moment.

3 **Provide a stamped addressed envelope.** If you're giving participants, say, a week to reflect on their experience of your training event, the stamp can have quite a pronounced psychological effect. An unreturned questionnaire becomes an unanswered letter!

4 **Run a raffle!** Number the questionnaires, and tell participants that the lucky winner will be chosen from all the replies you have by a named cut-off date. The prize could be a relevant learning package or book – or something much more imaginative.

5 **Consider using a very short 'instant' questionnaire, and a more spacious follow-up one a week later.** The second questionnaire could include questions about if and how participants' first reactions had changed on second thoughts.

6 **Global or selective?** Is it better to send it to fewer but more focused clients/groups or is it preferable to send it out more widely? This may of course depend on the topic. Will it be sent to specific people or a base/office for distribution? If the latter, ensure you have a named contact person who is willing to undertake the distribution and maybe the collection as well. Don't forget to allow reasonable time for people to reply.

7 **How is it to be analysed?** This may well depend upon the size of the questionnaire, and the facilities and finance available. Options include: by hand, or using an optical mark reader (OMR) for questionnaires where respondents put a pen or pencil mark in between strategically placed brackets. You may even be able to arrange for your questionnaire to be analysed by computer.

8 **Remember the performing dogs syndrome!** Some participants may happen to like you, and may want to give the responses they think you most want to see. Take more notice of the critical feedback than the positive feedback. Then sit back and *enjoy* the positive feedback!

9 **Think of unusual ways of distributing some questionnaires.** This will depend on the numbers involved, the turn-around time, the finance, staff and facilities at your disposal. Rather than just being given out at the end or sent by post, questionnaires could be sent by e-mail or the World Wide Web. They could be left in libraries, with the local doctor (with permission) or inside an in-house journal, local newspaper and so on.

10 **What to do afterwards?** We are now back to the beginning! What was the purpose of the questionnaire? Will the information you gain help with your planning of future seminars or training events? Will the information help you decide on future topics to offer? Will you now be able to target your clients more closely or extend your markets? Should you publish the outcomes of your research, or are they market-sensitive?

48

Following-up after a training event

Normally, fatigue and total relief (for us, anyway!) follow a training event. Once revived, however, we should ask ourselves: 'What next?'

1 **First, reflect.** A personal reflective journal is a really useful and essential tool. This may take the form of a notebook that you keep on one side, or a file in your container, or an audiotape you speak comments onto. The value lies not in the method of reflecting, but in the time taken doing so. Try and build in this time when planning a training event.

2 **Follow-up on the spot.** Ask your participants how they would like to keep in touch. If they are enthusiastic and feel that the training event was useful, they may ask you to organize a follow-up session, maybe in a month or even six months time. Try and set a date and place there and then if possible – you can always confirm or adjust later.

3 **Set an agenda.** It is really important that you have a proper agenda for a follow-up meeting. Write and confirm date, place and time as soon as possible. Then a week or two before the follow-up, write to participants with a draft agenda, and involve them as much as possible in fine-tuning it.

4 **Be clear about participants' involvement.** The greater the involvement of the group, the more your participants will take on ownership of the event. You may, for example, ask them to do presentations of what they have achieved since you last met. Give them an indication of how long you want these presentations to be, and the format you expect them to use. If you find they are not confident about the prospect of giving presentations, you have a clear pointer to the topic of a future training event!

5 **Set up local support or friendship groups.** These may be in one com-

pany, or within a geographical area. Think carefully about the purpose of such groups and how they will function. Do the groups need to establish ground rules – for example the frequency of their meetings?

6 **Think technologically.** Many organizations are now already connected (or thinking of being connected) by e-mail. This is a really quick and easy way of keeping in contact with many people in different places. A network can be set up so that one message automatically goes to every member of the group, allowing them to ask questions or reply individually at any time.

7 **Consider videoconferencing.** Almost by the minute, the price of videoconferencing is coming down. A computer, an ISDN telephone connection, special software and cameras, are all that we need. At the time of writing, if you already have the computer and telephone connection, the rest costs around £2,000.

8 **Consider a newsletter.** If you can produce a newsletter quickly and cheaply, it can provide an excellent way of keeping in touch with a group. With desk-top publishing, attractive looking newsletters can be produced very quickly. Plan the costings: who will pay for the paper, the printing and the distribution? The costs could be small, especially if the newsletter is kept to a single sheet of A4 paper.

9 **Don't forget audio-cassettes.** These are cheap, quick and easy to produce, and can provide an attractive way for members of a group to catch up with news and progress – for example while driving to work or commuting as passengers. They have the advantage of tone-of-voice and humanity. Also, the tapes can be re-used.

10 **Offer a qualification.** If your participants can obtain qualifications while attending your training events, so much the better. Find out about any related NVQs. Can you gain accreditation yourself as an assessor? Contact your local TEC (in the UK) for information and network details. Link in with local colleges or universities.

49

More ways of getting feedback!

A training event may be said to be successful if skills are developed and improvements are made to workplace performance, or participants' personal performance. But how can we find out exactly what changes take place as a direct result of our courses? The more different sources of feedback we can use, the better we can evaluate our courses.

1 **Clear aims are a must!** If we are to assess the success (or otherwise) of a course, we need to know what we hope to achieve. Ensure your group knows the aims. Also ensure that your participants' aims are identified and added to the agenda.

2 **How will participants know if they have been successful?** Ask them by what criteria they will know if they have succeeded, and who will be the judge – themselves, colleagues, line-managers, or a combination. This exercise provides useful information about how we as trainers can follow-up the outcomes of our courses.

3 **Get feedback from groups sometimes.** For example, giving a *group* a questionnaire to fill in collaboratively (or a report-back in open-ended form) allows the feedback you get to be informed by participants' discussions, rather than solely their individual feelings or views.

4 **Start a suggestion box.** Encourage participants to ask colleagues at all levels to list: one strength, one area for enhancement, and one aspect they think they have improved as a result of participating in your course. Then ask them to share this information with you and other group members. Make sensible ground rules for sensitive information.

5 **Set aside time for follow-up telephone calls to managers.** Time must be put in your diary if you are to gather feedback properly, and reflect on it well. If you intend to follow-up using the telephone, try to provide managers with a choice of times – they can't talk to you if they are busy or away. Suggest how long the conversation is likely to take, and stick to schedule. It can be a good idea to design a written checklist before you ring; this helps you to ask the same questions, and keeps you to target when side-tracked.

6 **Always allow time for, 'Is there anything else you would like to ask me or tell me?'** You'll often get some of the most valuable information in response to this final question in a telephone call.

7 **Set aside time for questionnaires.** Well-designed follow-up questionnaires can provide useful indications of changes that have occurred in people as a result of your course. Involving course participants in the design and distribution of questionnaires helps them set their own targets and focus their thinking.

8 **Can you accredit your course?** When this is possible, the results may indicate the degree of success of your training events. However, be cautious when interpreting success: many participants succeed despite their trainers. That said, a 100 per cent pass rate is usually a sure indication that the course went well.

9 **Try to find out about personal satisfaction and confidence.** Your participants may tell you one thing about these, but it's well worth finding out what they may have told other people. Use all opportunities to gently gather second-hand comments about your course from people your participants may have spoken to about it. Be careful not to appear to be 'spying' on your participants though – make it clear that the information you're seeking is for your benefit for future planning.

10 **Gain information from appraisal procedures.** For example, during a training event use a 'personal agenda setting' or 'personal action planning' exercise. Give participants time to design their own future targets, and suggest that they share these plans during appraisal interviews. Then ask them (or their managers) how useful the plans turned out to be.

50

Use managers in your evaluation

Gaining second-hand feedback of any sort is valuable, but finding out what your participants' line-managers discover about the effects of your training events is one of the most important sources of feedback.

1 **Find out who the managers are.** This can be done through a pre-course questionnaire, simply by asking for contact details regarding immediate line-managers. You may need to clarify that you're not intending to report back to managers about participants' performance – simply to find out from managers what they really want the course to achieve.

2 **Involve managers early.** The earlier you can involve your participants' managers the better. For example, encourage participants applying for your course or training event to obtain the signature of their boss or line-manager. At least then, these people know about who is attending – and you may find out who to ask about what the effects really were.

3 **Involve managers in the design of your training events.** Ask them for exact details of what they wish their staff to achieve as a result of your course, and make sure that the stated aims of the course embrace managers' requirements.

4 **Design good application forms.** Invite participants to list what they hope to achieve by attending your course, and how they will know that they've achieved it. Also ask them to explain how their line-manager will know whether they've been successful.

5 **Set follow-up work that involves line-managers.** Allow time during the training event for the participants to set themselves an activity which is to involve their line-manager in some way. It may be asking the manager to observe a task, or read a memo or minutes of a meeting, then to provide written or audio evidence that the task has been completed successfully and that feedback has been given to the participant.

6 **Encourage shared reflective journals.** Ongoing reflection allows us space to ask ourselves what went especially well and what future targets we want to set ourselves. Remember there is no such thing as failure – only feedback. Encourage participants to ask their managers directly for feedback. In journals, encourage participants to include comments from their managers, and to share such comments when appropriate with other group members.

7 **Encourage managers to come along and take part.** For example, where participants are looking at real work issues and coming up with action plans, get them to present their work to their own (or different) managers.

8 **Protect sensitive areas.** The sensitive nature of some issues may necessitate 'different' managers being invited instead of actual line managers. To ensure anonymity, individual issues could be shared with the group offering suggestions, then one issue could be chosen which they present to the rest. The invited manager need not know which person is involved. All these processes provide valuable staff development for managers themselves of course!

9 **Write your own special overall report for managers.** It helps to give them details of areas that you think remain to be achieved, not just catalogues of participants' successes!

10 **Run courses for managers themselves.** It can sometimes be worth conducting a *short* course for managers before running full courses for their staff. This helps the managers to know what you are trying to achieve, and also helps you find out much more about their expectations.

51

Replanning your training event

Very often, sooner or later you'll be running the same training event again. The best time to decide exactly how you'll make the next run of a training event better is while you're running your present one.

1 **Watch out for how your pre-event publicity really worked.** Look out for things that participants did not expect. Particularly be watchful for expectations your participants have that you had not thought of.

2 **Check how your arrangements actually worked.** When things go wrong at the venue, jot down some notes about how you could ensure that these particular things will not happen on a future occasion.

3 **Look for what worked well.** Often, things go well without any real planning. Try to ascertain the causes of things that go particularly well, and capitalize on these factors when planning your next similar training event.

4 **Ask yourself, 'What would I do differently in a similar situation tomorrow?'** Make notes of the changes you intend to make the next time you're planning to run a similar training session.

5 **Ask your participants, 'What should I stop?'** This direct question can provide you with some uncomfortable – but really useful – responses. If anyone thinks that some things you are doing are not useful or productive, it's worth thinking whether you can do something different next time.

6 **Ask your participants, 'What should I start next time?'** This can alert you to ways that you may be better able to meet the expectations or wishes of future participants on similar training events.

7   **Ask your participants, 'What should I continue doing in future?'** This is the good news! It's always useful to find out the things that your training event participants really appreciate or enjoy.

8   **Re-draft your training event programme immediately after the present event.** Don't trust that you will remember all the changes you may wish to make on the next occasion.

9   **When something just doesn't work, admit it!** Don't dig your heels in and say that it must remain part of your programme. Look for an alternative which may provide the same learning outcomes for your participants.

10 **Plan a new draft training event outline after every event.** These draft outlines can be the real ones you use as your event develops and evolves. Never be afraid to make changes. A programme that worked well once may work even better next time with changes.

Some Resources for Trainers

Blanchard, K and Johnson, S (1983) *The One Minute Manager*, William Collins, Glasgow.

Blanchard, K, Zigarmi, P, and Zigarmi, D (1987) *Leadership and the One Minute Manager*, William Collins, Glasgow.

Bourner, T, Martin, V and Race, P (1993) *Workshops that Work*, McGraw-Hill, Maidenhead.

Buzan, T (1988) *Make the Most of Your Mind*, Pan Books, London.

Buzan, T (1989) *Use Your Head*, BBC Books, London.

Buzan, T (1993) *The Mind Map Book: Radiant thinking*, BBC Publications, London.

Denny, R (1994) *Speak for Yourself*, Kogan Page, London.

De Porter, B and Hernacki, M (1993) *Quantum Learning: Unleash the genius within you*, Piatkus, London.

Ellington, H, Percival, F and Race, P (1993) *Handbook of Educational Technology (3rd Edition)*, Kogan Page, London.

Hargreaves, G (1993) *Managing Time: A practical guide to controlling your time*, BBC Training Videos, BBC Publications, London.

Hoff, R (1992) *I Can See You Naked*, Andrews and McMeel, Kansas, USA.

McCann, D (1988) *How to Influence Others at Work*, Heinemann, Oxford.

Race, P (1994) *Never Mind the Teaching – Feel the Learning*, SEDA Publications, Birmingham.

Rawlins, K (1993) *Presentation and Communication Skills*, Macmillan Magazines, London.

Thomson, P (1994) *Conversation and the Power of Persuasion*, Nightingale Conant, Paignton.

Trulove, S (ed) (1992) *Handbook of Training and Development*, Blackwell, Oxford.

Questionnaire

(Your feedback to Phil and Brenda!)

1   Please tell us which tips you personally found most useful.
    (To save time, you can simply jot the numbers down, eg 10/1 for the
    first tip in set number 10, and so on.)

2   Please tell us about any tips which you think we should definitely
    ditch!

3   What do you think about the tone and style of this book?

4   Please give us suggestions about how we can improve the next edition
    of this book.

5   If you would like to contribute some further tips for the next edition,
    please jot them below (or on separate paper).

Include your name and address please, so we can acknowledge you.

Index